Anonymous

The True Psalmody

The Bible Psalms the Church's Only Manual of Praise - with prefaces by Henry Cooke, John Edgar, and Thomas Houston

Anonymous

The True Psalmody
The Bible Psalms the Church's Only Manual of Praise - with prefaces by Henry Cooke, John Edgar, and Thomas Houston

ISBN/EAN: 9783337126674

Printed in Europe, USA, Canada, Australia, Japan

Cover: Foto ©Lupo / pixelio.de

More available books at **www.hansebooks.com**

THE
TRUE PSA[LMODY;]

OR,

THE BIBLE PSALMS T[HE]
ONLY MANUAL O[F ...]

WITH PREF[ACE]
BY THE
H[EN]RY COO[K]E, D.D., LL.D., R[...]
AND
[T]HOMAS H[...]

BELFAST:
[...] PUBLISHED BY JAMES JOHNSTON.
[...]B, C. AITCHISON, AND M. POLLOCK, BELFAST; D. ROBERTSON,
[AN]D CURRY AND CO., DUBLIN; R. HAMILTON, LONDONDERRY;
A. ELLIOT, EDINBURGH; GEO. GALLIE, GLASGOW;
ALEX. GARDENER, PAISLEY.

1861.

ENTERED AT STATIONERS' HALL.

PREFACE

BY THE

REV. HENRY COOKE, D.D., LL.D.

Having been requested to write a Preface to a reprint, in Ireland, of an American treatise on the Psalmody of Christian worship, I have most cheerfully complied;—partly on account of the importance of the subject—partly on account of the talent displayed in the work—and partly that, by a detail of my own experience, I may add my humble testimony to a great principle.

My earliest recollection of family and public psalmody is that of the exclusive use of the English version of the Biblical Psalms, authorized by the Reformed Church of Scotland. In our Presbyterian Churches, so far as my knowledge extends, others were unknown. When I entered the ministry, in 1807, the Scottish selection of Paraphrases and Hymns had come into partial use; and influenced by the feeling in their favour, I was gradually led to adopt them. The principle of their use once adopted, the way to others was opened to an unlimited extent; for, if these paraphrases and hymns be good for public worship, it follows that others may be as good, or better. Accordingly, at one time of my ministry, I dedicated both time and pains to selecting, from all accessible sources, an additional volume, with an essay, embodying a defence of its use in private or in public worship. I need scarcely add, that I believed

PREFACE.

my arguments—which were partly original, and partly derivative—to be unanswerable.

I shall now detail, and as briefly as may be, the circumstances that first led me to doubt, and finally to reject my former conclusions.

Having been appointed to a short missionary tour, I left my home in good health, but was taken suddenly ill, and, during a month, was unable to return; and it was when " wearisome nights were appointed to me, and tossings to and fro until the dawning of the day," that, in frequent solitude, I was thrown, almost entirely, on the resources of memory. But with that faculty God had sufficiently endowed me; and the psalms committed in school-boy days, and paraphrases and hymns of riper years, presented ready subjects of meditation. And it was then, that, all unexpectedly, yet irresistibly, it was impressed upon me, by experience and feeling, that the most celebrated hymns of uninspired men were, like Job's friends, "miserable comforters," when compared with the experience of Christ, in the days of humiliation, of which the Book of Psalms is the true prophetic picture.

And here I think it right to record the circumstances by which I was led to discover what I believe to be the true key to unlock the door of the psalms. In common with many of my brethren in the ministry, I had been accustomed to explain the morning psalm before singing, and, I believe, in common also with many, to interpret such psalms as the First (v. 1, 2, 3), and the Twenty-fourth (v. 3, 4) as elevated and elevating descriptions—not of what a believer has attained, or, in this life, can attain to, but of what he should always endeavour to attain. This canon of interpretation was almost constantly in use. Now the mind is seldom satisfied with an erroneous principle; mine, in this case, was not; for it seemed still a species of fiction. Yet I could not see my way to a better, and no man of my counsel led me. But I thought—I waited—and prayed for light; and the manner of my enlightenment was this. I had formerly, to some extent, studied botany and mineralogy; and was occasionally renewing my studies. During an excursion, a learned friend presented me a wild flower, and told me its name. I showed him another, and he could not name it. In colour and in form, it was very like the flower he had showed me, and I suggested a name derived from this partial similarity. But my friend, without hesitation, pronounced against the name, as the two plants, though like in some respects, essentially differed in others. A dear brother in Christ had lent me a new work of descriptive mineralogy, and we had compared specimens with descriptions; I often found it difficult to determine the name, though some of the external characters of the minerals agreed with the book. One principle, however, was adopted in all my enquiries and decisions: the mineral and the book must exactly agree. Now, it was after having attempted to explain the verses referred to in the Twenty-fourth Psalm; and when I was in the act of explaining, as best I could, the First Psalm, and while labouring to accommodate the description in the psalm with the state of all I knew of the attainments of the saints, that it occurred to me to say in my heart—is this the way we decide in botany and mineralogy? and my memory and my conscience answered no! Then said I, in my heart, there never has been a man answering, in all respects, to these descriptions. It was not Adam—Noah—Abraham—Moses—Paul; but was it not "the man Christ Jesus?" The veil was instantly removed from the Book of Psalms, and I saw therein Christ clearly. He was the man of the First Psalm—the man of the Twenty-fourth—the man of nearly the whole book. Now, while I set not up my own convictions as a rule or measure of the consciences of others, I cannot fail to pity those who can find, as they assert, so little of Christ in the inspired psalmody of the Bible, that they must seek and employ an uninspired psalmody as exhibiting Him more fully. Our Lord Himself found Himself in the psalms—(Luke xxiv. 44, 45)—and thereby "opened His disciples' understanding, that they might understand the Scriptures." Surely what was the clearest light to *their* eyes, should be light to *ours*. And, truly, I believe, there is one view of Christ—and that not the least important to the tired and troubled believer—that can be discovered only in the Book of Psalms—I mean His inward life. No eye-witness of the outward man—though an inspired evangelist—could penetrate the heart. But the Spirit who "searcheth the deep things of God," has, in the psalms, laid open the inmost thoughts, sorrows, and conflicts of our Lord. The Evangelists faithfully and intelligently depict the sinless Man; the psalms alone lay open the heart of "the Man of sorrows." The most pious productions of uninspired men are a shallow stream—the psalms an unfathomable and shoreless ocean.

PREFACE.

In conclusion, I beg to record, that two things confirmed my decision in favour of the exclusive use of inspired psalmody in public worship. First, the Biblical Psalms being inspired by the Holy Ghost, (2 Tim. iii. 16; 1 Peter i. 21), in using them, there can be no error. Secondly, though in uninspired sacred poetry I had discovered many beauties and other excellencies, I never had discovered any compilations which I could pronounce free from serious doctrinal errors. This I perceived to be especially the case with not a few of the Paraphrases and Hymns, authorized by the Church of Scotland. If a doctrinal error be, at all times, dangerous, how much more when it is stereotyped in the devotions of the sanctuary!

H. COOKE.

Belfast, *April, 8th,* 1861.

PREFACE

BY THE

REV. JOHN EDGAR, D.D., LL.D.

I HEARTILY approve of the re-publication of the American volume entitled "THE TRUE PSALMODY." The eminent names associated with its publication in the United States are a sufficient guarantee for its Scriptural character and genuine worth. It contains an invaluable amount of sound criticism, unanswerable argument, and historic research. In a spirit truly Christian, and with resistless force of truth, it discusses and settles "THE CHURCH'S ONLY MANUAL OF PRAISE."

It is the right book at the right time. It will greatly strengthen and comfort pious spirits, who have been vexed by the obtrusive confidence and flippant assertion of "them that are given to change." They will be built up and established in their most holy faith, "abounding therein with thanksgiving," by a complete vindication of the perfect book of inspired psalms, from calumnies heaped on it by hymn-singers, under pretext of pouring contempt on the Scottish version, prepared by the Westminster Assembly, and, after earnest examination and repeated revision, appointed to be used in the public and family worship of the Church of Scotland.

Trashy rhymes, called hymns (though often not even rhyme), have long been a sore infliction, and have too long, alas! and too largely, usurped the place of inspired psalms. It is full time that, in all public worship, God's own book of sacred song should occupy the place to which it was divinely appointed, and for which it alone is qualified. It is full of Christ, full of heavenly gospel truth, and of sublime expressions of adoring praise, worthy of the only object of all religious praise to dictate and to receive.

Christian experience and taste have been degraded by the frivolous, empty, puny things—puny in expression, and barren in thought—with which, under the name of hymns, different sections of the church have been enfeebled and deluged. The Chairman of the committee on psalmody, in the most influential church of the New World, honestly confessed that, after having read six or seven times their revised book of hymns, he thought it "the meanest book he had ever seen."

It is sad to think how, under a profession of enlarging the sphere of sacred song, it has, by the intrusion of human writings, been wretchedly curtailed; and that, with a countless gathering of compositions from Romish, Unitarian, and similar sources—whether from the pen of Watts, who wished to see "David converted into a Christian," or Logan, or Romish Pope, or Moore, or Miss Martineau, the issue has extensively been the exclusion of praise entirely from the worship of God, except as conducted by an organ and hired choir.

The Scottish version of the psalms is not perfect, nor is the English translation of the Bible; but both are so near perfection, and so interwoven with Christian faith and feeling, that it is a question of the gravest character whether either of them should be changed. Independent of inspiration and the highest sanctions, and of very many tender, holy, and sublime associations, the Book of Psalms, in the Scottish version, is incomparably superior to any book of sacred song that the world ever saw. To my own heart it is very dear; to my own ear it is poetic, spiritual, and sublime; and in my own mind, it is associated with the sunniest memories of the sacred past, recalling testimonies to its excellence from those who sing now before the throne, and triumphant quotations from its heavenly pages, as I drew the last curtain round the bed of death.

JOHN EDGAR, D.D.

PREFACE

BY THE
REV. THOMAS HOUSTON, D.D.

BRETHREN in America of different religious denominations—the excellent men who agreed to emit this able defence of Scriptural Psalmody, have performed a valuable service to the cause of true religion by its publication. In their own country, they have had a full opportunity of testing by its fruits the practice of departing from an inspired psalmody, and of introducing at will into the worship of the church hymns of human composition. In no part of reformed Christendom has there been a wider license taken in the use of hymns of all kinds—some evangelical, others abounding in doctrinal error, and many inflated and extravagant—in public psalmody; and this not only among the newly arisen sects, but likewise in those that profess adherence to ancient standards, such as the Episcopal and Presbyterian Churches. The consequences have been, amidst much that is praiseworthy and commendable in the American Churches, divisions have been multiplied, errors in new forms have been brought in—and in many, fanatical and dangerous excitement has been encouraged—while doctrinal truth and Scriptural order have been disregarded. It is significant and striking too, that what are termed the "Psalm-singing Churches" in America have been generally preserved united in evangelical sentiment, and kept from the disorders and confusions into which others have fallen; while, it is believed, they will compare advantageously with others, in relation to the strict observance of moral and religious duties—to efforts for the extension of the Redeemer's kingdom—and in all the visible fruits of genuine piety.

The Committee of Presbyterian Ministers and Elders that compiled "THE TRUE PSALMODY"—all of them distinguished men in the several Bodies with which they are connected—aware of such facts, set themselves to provide a remedy for existing and wide-spread evils, and to lift up a faithful testimony in behalf of precious truth. Ably have they accomplished the task which they undertook; and the church, not only in America, but also in other countries, owes them a debt of gratitude, for the full, Scriptural, and candid vindication which they have presented of the purity of one of her most important institutions. Overlooking a few references to practices that are American and local, and without considering ourselves called to adopt every exposition or argument that is offered by such a multitude of authors as are quoted, we regard this work as admirably fitted for general circulation, and the matter contained in it as of more than ordinary interest to all who love the truth, desire to promote the unity and peace of the church, and to advance the cause of vital godliness.

To "contend earnestly" for purity of worship, is an important duty, at all times, solemnly and frequently enjoined in the Divine word; and, in the present day of religious inquiry—of sudden and unexpected changes—and of the revival and spread of fundamental errors, it is especially incumbent. The rejection of human inventions in the worship of God, was a main plea of the noble Puritans; and in maintaining it, our Presbyterian and Covenanting forefathers willingly suffered imprisonment, exile, and death. Their grand principle was, that nothing but what is of express Scriptural warrant should be admitted in the order and devotions of the sanctuary. In this they were clearly right. All true revival and reform in past ages have proceeded more or less on the same principle; and, in the promised future period of the church's enlargement and prosperity, we are assured, that all will-worship, as well as superstition and error, shall be purged out; and that Mount Zion shall appear, in renovated light and purity, the joy of all the earth—the "habitation of justice, and mountain of holiness."

Uninspired hymns and paraphrases to supplement or supplant the Bible Psalms, were first introduced amid declension from the truth, and have been often resorted to for the purpose of ministering to extravagant excitement. Though many good men have been misled by a prevailing practice, their employment in the church psalmody has ever been fraught with serious evils. God's word has been dishonoured—the songs of inspiration have been displaced from the use for which they were given—low and unworthy views of inspiration have been countenanced—and men have presumptuously set up their own wisdom above God's. Addictedness to hymn-singing ministers to false excitement, causes or perpetuates divisions in the church, and completely mars the prospect of a happy union in truth and love—one of the grand promises to the church in the last times.

PREFACE.

The open and candid discussion of the question of inspired Psalmody has, in various places, and at different times, been productive of no little good. Of this there is a striking instance in the history of one of the works which is frequently quoted in "THE TRUE PSALMODY." When the Rev. William Sommerville, some thirty years ago, landed as a missionary from this country in Nova Scotia, he found the inspired psalms almost wholly excluded from the worship of all sections of the Protestant Church in that country; and hymns of all sorts, many of them erroneous, trashy, and insipid, in general use among Presbyterians, Methodists, Baptists, Universalists, &c. His frequent and able advocacy of the Bible Psalms, and especially the publication of his work on "THE EXCLUSIVE CLAIMS OF DAVID'S PSALMS," produced a marked change of sentiment on the subject throughout the religious community; and now, among Presbyterians of every name in Nova Scotia, the use of the inspired psalms in the worship of God, public and domestic, is as general as was that of mere human compositions before. The issuing of an edition of "THE TRUE PSALMODY" in this country, and its extensive circulation, will, there is reason to hope, be productive of like beneficial effects. Under the Divine blessing, I anticipate no little advantage from its perusal, in leading many throughout the churches to views on the subject, of which they have hitherto been profoundly ignorant, in exciting to farther inquiry, and the rejection of other corruptions from the church; and thus, in preparing for the desired and blissful era, when "the watchmen shall see eye to eye, and with the voice together they shall sing," as "the Lord shall bring again Zion."

PREFACE.

The testimony of the excellent commentator, Thomas Scott, respecting the Bible Psalms, at once judicious and weighty, finds a response in the heart of every faithful and devoted Christian who is familiar with these songs of Zion—"There is nothing in true religion—doctrinal, experimental, and practical—but will present itself to our attention whilst we meditate upon the Psalms. The Christian's use of them in the closet, and the minister's in the pulpit, will generally increase with the growing experience of the power of true religion in their own hearts."

THOMAS HOUSTON.

KNOCKBRACKEN, *May*, 1861.

INTRODUCTION TO FIRST EDITION.

The celebration of God's praise in song, and with the "voice of melody," is among the most delightful of religious exercises. It is the natural expression of holy confidence and joy in God : "Is any merry? let him sing psalms;" "They shall come with singing unto Zion, and everlasting joy shall be upon their heads." It is in singing praises that the united voices of the worshippers of God are heard in Christian assemblies. While thus engaged, if ever, the heart is stirred and moved to penitential emotion, to adoring homage, to grateful thanksgiving, to lofty hopes and anticipations. Whatever relates to such an exercise and ordinance must be of no minor importance. Above all, the inquiry, What shall be the *matter* of our praise? What sacred songs shall we sing? must be of the very highest moment. We may naturally, and with the deepest interest, ask, whether the Most High has Himself provided us with a manual of praise? or, has He left us to make or gather songs, other than He has furnished, as we may have the ability, or make our choice?

Whatever the result of our examination of these inquiries—and, it is but too well known, all have not reached the same conclusions,—none can deny that they are worthy of our most devout and earnest attention. For—

1. We serve a "jealous God" who claims as His inalienable prerogative, the designation and appointment of all that relates to religious worship. "In vain do they worship me, teaching for doctrines the commandments of men." And, surely, those who draw nigh to God in acts of devotion, should be as deeply concerned now, as of old, lest they be found to offer "strange fire before the Lord." In every part and act of worship we should endeavour to be well assured that we approach the throne of the Eternal with a service which he has prescribed, and which, presented in faith, He will accept. And thus ("For the Lord, whose name is Jealous, is a jealous God," Ex. xxxiv. 14), whether a prayer, a doctrine, or a psalm, it is a solemn inquiry, It is according to the will of God?

Is it not enough that our offering, or the manner in which we present it, seem to *us* well adapted to awaken pious emotion, or develop Christian affections. This is one of the most marked, and most baneful of the errors of that system of corrupt Christianity which the entire Protestant world rejects as Antichristian: and hence, its pictures, its images, its gorgeous and impressive ceremonial — "having a show of wisdom," but, after all, only "in will-worship" (Col. ii. 22), unacceptable to God, unprofitable to the worshipper, and, at last, fatal to the interests of vital religion and personal piety.

Adopt this principle, and where shall we fix its limits? If human ingenuity once begin to meddle with the devotions of the people of God, where shall it be arrested? where *can* it be arrested? Hence, with wise and beneficent forethought, as well as with a jealous regard to His own glory, as the church's only King and Head, our God and Saviour has excluded from His church every invention of man; has stamped upon every institution and ordinance the impress of His own sovereign and most gracious authority. He has left us but the office and the privilege of studying His word, that we may ascertain His will, and then follow it with a jealousy and vigilance like His own.

2. The psalmody of the church has no feeble influence upon her doctrines, and upon the tone and spirit of her piety. An eminent statesman of the old world once remarked, "Let me make the ballads of a nation, and I care not who makes its laws." A nation's songs do certainly mould, if not to so great an extent as this apophthegm would imply, yet, very largely indeed, the sentiments, the feelings, and even the opinions of its citizens. The songs of the church, sung from day to day, from Sabbath to Sabbath, cannot but influence, at least as widely and profoundly, her tone of feeling, and her religious views. Expressing, as they will necessarily do, in the first instance, something of the principles, the spirit, the prominent desires and aims of those who adopt them as the matter of their praise, they must react with no little energy and efficacy upon the hearts of the worshippers as they thus use them. They impress their image deeply by constant use and consequent familiarity. Hence, it occurs, by no means unfrequently, that songs composed by uninspired poets, acquire in the estimation of those who have long employed them in their devotions, a character, little, if any, less sacred than that which attaches to the word of God itself. How infinitely important then, to have every assurance that our "Psalmody" be not only sound in doctrine, but Christ-like in tone, spirit, and sentiment! How high the responsibility resting upon those who take upon themselves to frame and establish a church's songs of devotion!

3. The Church's Psalmody should be fixed, stable, permanent. Like her faith, it should be, as nearly as possible, unchanging. Intimately associated as it is with her spiritual life, the matter of her praise should not be liable to fluctuate and change with

the fickle movements of public sentiment, and the vacillations which ever mark the tastes of human society. Her faith is "one" (Eph. iv. 5); her songs should also be ever the same. It is something here, moreover, to be identified with the worthies and witnesses of the past in singing the same psalms which have sustained and cheered the saints of God, and faithful servants of Christ in their day of trial and of death; and something more that our children after us become identified with us, not only in perusing the same Bible, in loving the same Saviour, in seeking the same salvation, but also in singing at the domestic altar, in their social and public assemblies, and in gathering around the table of the Lord, the same sacred songs.

Our answer to the inquiries which have been suggested, has, no doubt, been already anticipated. We believe, most firmly, that we have been provided with a manual of praise in that part of the Holy Scriptures styled "The Book of Psalms," and that this, to the exclusion of all uninspired songs, should be in a literal translation, sung in the worship of God. For the reasons which constitute the grounds of our faith in this matter, we refer the reader to the sequel of this volume. We may,.however, premise a few general reflections. And 1. In using "The Book of Psalms," we are on safe ground. It is a part of the inspired Scriptures: of course, like other parts of the same sacred volume, indited by the Spirit of Christ (2 Sam. xxiii. 2, 1 Pet. i. 11, 2 Pet. i. 21), and as such must be immaculate in doctrine, and right in tone and spirit. It is permanent. Whatever changes time and the consequent various usage of language may render necessary in the words of a given translation, the book itself is a portion of that word of God which "abideth for ever." While other systems of psalmody—the composures of men—are ever changing, this remains to instruct and edify the saints of God throughout all generations. Once appointed of God to be sung in celebrating His praise, we can now employ its language with no apprehension that He will meet us with the alarming inquiry, "Who hath required this at your hands?"

2. In advocating the exclusive use of "The Book of Psalms" we advocate the cause of Christian Union. We well know, indeed, that diversity of judgment and of practice in this matter is not the only occasion and source of ecclesiastical separation, but it is one of the roots of this baneful Upas. And, in so far as disunion does arise from this cause, how shall it cease? upon what basis shall we meet? We can see no other than that of a psalmody which presents this high claim—that it is the acknowledged gift of God himself to men. Were it ever so, that we were warranted to make each his own songs, and sing them, surely we cannot claim the right to impose these upon

INTRODUCTION.

our brethren, or compel them to sit silent in our religious assemblies! Concession—if there must be concession—should, by all means, come from those who, at most, can only claim *permission*—who do not even profess, if we understand them, to possess in their favour divine *institution:* who cannot assert, at any rate, that *their* compositions bear the direct and unmistakeable impress of Christ's authority: an impress so clear, that he who refuses to use them, limiting himself to the inspired Psalms, is guilty of despising an ordinance of Christ. Here, then, is a common, because a Bible ground, on which, so far as one great and prominent cause of division is concerned, we may meet and harmonize.

This consideration should, we think, address itself with peculiar force to the churches which trace their origin to the Reformation Church in the British Islands. Our fathers were once united in singing praise to God in the psalms of the Bible. Why are their descendants, so many of them, now severed in this matter of praising God? There can be but one reply. By the introduction into the worship of God of songs of human composition, or of psalms which profess to be no more than "imitations" of those of the Bible. How, then, is this cause of separation and alienation to be removed? By the universal return to the one, definite, permanent, and safe basis—the psalms indited by the Holy Ghost. We are well satisfied that *we* are not chargeable with perpetuating schism, because we adhere in our praises to the very matter provided for us by Him whose praises we celebrate.

But are there not already before the Church able and excellent works advocating our views in this respect? There are. We gratefully acknowledge the fact, but still feel ourselves justified in adding another volume to the list. These works are now mostly difficult of access, because chiefly out of the market: some of them are in the form of criticisms upon essays, &c., defending human compositions; some of them are written, and wisely, with an eye to local circumstances—all have their peculiar excellencies, which we aim at combining, as far as possible in one volume.

In this last remark, we indicate the character of the following work: it is largely a *compilation;* and we have made free use of the remarks of Tholuck in the introduction to his Commentary on the Psalms, and have quoted on some points largely from the works of Rev. Wm. Sommerville, of Nova Scotia; of Dr. Pressly, of Allegheny; of Mr. Gordon, and of Dr. M'Master. The criticism on Col. iii. 16, is from the pen of Dr. Cooper, of this city. In all cases, our quotations are distinguished by the marks usually employed, while throughout we have introduced, as was judged seasonable, other arguments and answers to

INTRODUCTION.

objections not noticed or fully considered, according to our views, elsewhere, and also the necessary connecting links: for these the chairman of the committee is chiefly responsible. Thoroughly satisfied that the subject is one that eminently deserves careful investigation, we commend this effort to vindicate principles which we regard as most important to the purity and unity of the Christian church, to the devout and prayerful examination of the candid inquirer after truth and duty, and to the blessing of Him who "inhabiteth the praises of Israel."

NOTE.

THE ministers and elders of the Reformed and United Presbyterian Churches of Philadelphia, believing that the times demand a full presentation of the subject herein discussed, held a meeting in the Cherry Street Church, Aug. 16th, 1858, at which Revs. J. M. Willson, J. T. Cooper, and Robert J. Black, were appointed a Committee to prepare, from existing treatises, a work in favour of the exclusive use of the Scripture Psalmody as the matter of the Church's praise. Rev. William Sterret was subsequently added to the Committee. At an adjourned meeting, having presented an outline of the work, the Committee were unanimously authorized to proceed with its publication. The names of the ministers present are as follows:— Revs. J. M. Willson, S. O. Wylie, David M'Kee, William Sterret, Robert J. Black, S. P. Herron, A. G. M'Auley, Francis Church, J. B. Dales, D.D., J. T. Cooper, D.D., G. C. Arnold, Robert Armstrong, and T. H. Beveridge. Elders:—Robert Orr, John Evans, R. Skilton, Wm. Blakely, Dr. A. S. M'Murray, Henry Floyd, William Crawford, William Brown, and others.

FRANCIS CHURCH, *Chairman.*
G. C. ARNOLD, *Secretary.*

CONTENTS.

	PAGE
PREFACE BY THE REV. HENRY COOKE, D.D., LL.D.,	3
PREFACE BY THE REV. JOHN EDGAR, D.D., LL.D.,	8
PREFACE BY THE REV. THOMAS HOUSTON, D.D.,	11
INTRODUCTION TO FIRST EDITION,	17

CHAPTER I.

THE BOOK OF PSALMS A COMPLETE MANUAL OF PRAISE.

Presents the most comprehensive delineation of the perfections of God, and of the character of His government—In Three Persons—Furnishes a full and accurate exhibition of man's real state and character before God—The Psalms are full of Christ—Contain the richest fund of Christian experience—The most eminent Christians and Christian teachers have ever so testified, ... 33

CHAPTER II.

THE BOOK OF PSALMS HAS THE SEAL OF DIVINE APPOINTMENT, WHICH NO OTHER HAS.

Divinely appointed—No other Psalms have such appointment—The Church of Christ, one under both Testaments, ... 55

CHAPTER III.

NO WARRANT FOR MAKING OR USING ANY OTHER HYMNS IN THE WORSHIP OF GOD.

I. *Arguments used in behalf of such warrant*—That Scripture sanctions it—That hymns have the sanction of long and extensive use in the church—The argument from analogy, from the use of our own words in prayer—A part of our Christian liberty—Used by godly men

CONTENTS.

Hymns may be read, &c., with edification. *II. Arguments against the use of Hymns*—None but inspired Psalms used during the Old Testament economy—There is no authority by which we can be called upon to sing hymns—The use of hymns sets aside the Psalms—Hymns are sectarian—It has been found impracticable to frame an acceptable and permanent book of hymns—The advocacy of hymns has led to great errors—The use of hymns has led to the abandonment very largely of congregational and family singing in praise of God, ... 73

CHAPTER IV.

OBJECTIONS TO THE USE OF THE PSALMS CONSIDERED.

That they speak of a Saviour to come—That they are encumbered with Old Testament allusions, &c.—That they are not adapted to a revival of religion—That they are hard to understand—That they are unsuitable for children—That the Psalms are not adapted to the condition of every worshipper—That Churches which use hymns are more prosperous than such as do not—That the spirit of some of the Psalms is unchristian—If we use the Psalms, why not sing the titles, &c.? 148

CHAPTER V.

REMARKS UPON THE "SCOTTISH VERSION" OF THE PSALMS.

It has been subjected to the most careful examination as to its fidelity—It may claim to be a faithful rendering—"Imitations" of the Psalms are to be compared with it in this respect—It has been largely approved by men of acknowledged taste, though, of course, susceptible of improvement, as is our English Bible, ... 167

APPENDIX, ... 171

THE TRUE PSALMODY.

THE BIBLE PSALMS THE MATTER OF THE CHURCH'S PRAISE.

CHAPTER I.

THE BOOK OF PSALMS IS A COMPLETE MANUAL OF PRAISE.

I. *It presents the most comprehensive delineation of the perfections of God, and of the character of His government.* "Here," in the words of Tholuck, "is God praised, who, before the mountains, the earth, and the world had been created, is from everlasting to everlasting—who surrounds His creatures, inquiring everywhere—whose presence cannot be avoided, whether in heaven above or the depth below—from whom darkness cannot hide—who reigns as the Lord omnipotent, from the beginning, in the heavens—who thunders in His might—who telleth the number of the stars, and calleth them all by their names—who is good unto all, has compassion on all His works, and giveth food to the young ravens which cry—who delighteth not in the strength of the horse nor the legs of a man, but taketh pleasure in them that fear Him and hope in His mercy—who, like as a father pitieth his children, pitieth those that fear Him, and dealeth not with us after our sins, nor rewardeth us according to our iniquities. Whatever truths and praises can be said of the wisdom, eternity, omnipotence, holiness, and mercy of God, are expressed in the Psalms, such as Psalms xc., xci., xcvii., xxxiii., ciii., civ., and cxxxix. Here is a piety which, on the one hand losing itself full of praise in the care of God, as in Psalm cxix., preserves on the other a clear and opened eye for His glory in nature, before whose view the declaration in the book of the law and that in the book of nature entirely commingle. (Psalm xix.) Here we have the unceasing praise of God—in gloomy as well as in joyous days, for mercies temporal and spiritual—in every variety of tone and expression. The last Psalms (cxlvii., cxlviii., and cl.), the many-toned echo of the entire book, or like the end of a long chain, call, with their unceasing 'Praise ye the Lord,' upon Israel and all mankind, the heights and the depths and the heavenly spirits, to offer the sacrifice of their praise to the Lord. Those who adhere to the erroneous opinion (Psalms xxix., civ., cxlv.) that the God of Israel was the God of the nation only in that sense, that the people believed, besides Him, in other though impotent heathen deities, may derive more correct views from the Psalms. 'For God is the King *of all the earth:* sing ye praises with understanding. God reigneth over *the heathen:* God sitteth upon the throne of His holiness.' (Psalm xlvii. 7, 8.) 'O God of our salvation, *who art the confidence of all the ends of the earth, and of them that are afar off upon the sea.*' (Psalm lxv. 5.) 'Among the gods there is none like unto thee, O Lord; neither are there any works like unto thy works. All nations whom thou hast made shall come and worship before thee, O Lord, and shall glorify thy name. For thou art great, and doest wondrous things: *thou art God alone.*' (Psalm lxxxvi. 8—10). Contrasted with the gods of the heathen, which are less than their worshippers, which have eyes and see not, and ears and hear not, the God of Israel appears as the living God, who governs the world, and that in *righteousness;* who maintaineth the right and cause of the innocent, and sitteth enthroned as the righteous Judge (Psalm ix. 5); who throweth the ungodly into a ditch, and causeth their desire to perish (Psalm vii. 17; cxii. 10); who preserveth the soul of His saints, and delivereth them out of the hand of the wicked (Psalm xcvii. 10); who heareth the cry of the righteous (Psalm xxxiv. 18); delivereth them out of all trouble, and maketh their eyes see their desire upon their enemies (Psalm liv. 9); who causeth the godly to prosper in whatsoever he doeth. (Psalm i. 3.). In a word, these Psalms express the truths, so manifest and momentous, that the government of the one true God, of even this world which He has himself created, is based on justice—that evil is ever condemned by its inflexible laws—that its condemnation will sooner or later be visible to all in heaven and on earth, while to all 'light is sown for the righteous, and gladness for the upright in heart.'" (Ps. xcvii. 2.)*

II. *The Living God is praised in these Psalms as subsisting in Three Persons, Father, Son, and Holy Ghost.* We here adopt the language of Mr. Gordon. "Three persons in one Godhead, Father, Son, and Holy Ghost, is the God to whom they ascribe praise. If it could be shown that they spoke only of the Father, and of Him obscurely, it would be a very weighty objection against employing them in Christian worship; for the glorious mystery of the Trinity is most clearly revealed to us, and ought to enter into our praises. But nothing is more evident than this, that the object of all their ascriptions is, Three in One. It cannot be denied that they employ the name *Jehovah* in the sense in which it is used in other parts of Scripture; and every one who believes the doctrine of the Trinity will admit that this name is applied to each of the persons. This much will show that a trinity of persons is discernible in the Psalms. But we find each of the three persons particularly mentioned: 'He shall cry unto me, Thou art my Father, my God, and the Rock of my salvation.' (Ps. lxxxix. 25.) Upon reading the Psalm carefully over, it will appear that the speaker in this verse is God the Father, the first person of the Trinity. The person

* Tholuck's Com. on Psalms, pp. 33, 34.

spoken of is called David. God showed great mercy unto David, and conferred many remarkable blessings upon him; admitted him to great nearness, and gave him a very high character: he was a man according to God's own heart; yet it will be impossible to find a proper application for all that is here said, in *his* history. Many things are here said that cannot be predicated of any creature, viz.: 'Thy seed will I establish for ever, and build up thy throne to all generations.' 'Then thou spakest in vision to thy Holy One, and saidst, I have laid help on one that is mighty: he shall cry, Thou art my Father.' 'I will make him my first-born, higher than kings of any land. His seed also will I make to endure for ever, and his throne as the days of heaven.' But to Him who was David's son according to the flesh, and who is often in Scripture called David, they will apply with the utmost propriety; and of Him are they spoken. Here, then, are the Father and the Son both mentioned.

"In the 47th Psalm, the Holy Ghost calls to shout with the voice of triumph; and the reason He assigns for it is, 'God has gone up with a shout; the Lord with the sound of a trumpet.' Then He calls on the church to break forth in rapture: 'Sing praise to God; sing praise, sing praise unto our King; sing praises, for God is King of all the earth; sing praises with understanding; God reigneth over the heathen.' To no event other than the ascension and inauguration of Christ to His throne can this passage possibly be applied. When God, in human nature, went up to the third heavens, in triumph over His enemies, He went up as King of all the earth; for all power both in heaven and earth was given into His hand; and He was, by a special relation, King of the church. He went up with a right to take possession of the heathen as His inheritance. So that every circumstance perfectly agrees with this description; and we conclude with a full conviction that it is God the Son, incarnate, who is here receiving the praise of the church. The same event is described in the 68th, from the 18th verse to the end, where solemn praise is offered up unto Christ as Lord. And the proper application of this passage is settled in Eph. iv. 7.

"In the 2d Psalm, the ineffable Sonship is expressed: 'Thou art my Son; this day have I begotten thee.'* In the 45th, His Deity and the eternity of His kingdom are asserted: 'Thy throne, O God, is for ever and ever.'†

"In the 102d, creating power is ascribed unto the Son: 'And thou, Lord, in the beginning, hast laid the foundations of the earth; the heavens also are the works of thy hands.'‡

"In the 51st, the Holy Ghost is introduced: 'Take not thy Holy Spirit away; stay me with thy free Spirit.'

"In the 104th, creating power is ascribed to Him: 'Thou sendest forth thy *Spirit*, they are *created*.' And in the 139th we are taught to ascribe omniscience to Him: 'Whither shall I go from thy Spirit, or flee from thy presence?'"§

III. *The Psalms furnish a full and accurate exhibition of man's natural state and character before God, and in contrast with His ineffable majesty and holiness*: thus summed up by the same eminent writer from whom we have already quoted: "Our apprehension of the majesty and holiness of God should be accompanied by a sense of our own nothingness and sin." The Psalmist, alluding to the statement in Genesis, speaks of man as *made a little lower than God* (Luther), that God hath put all things under His feet, and glories in the fact that man, though externally more helpless than any other creature, does by virtue of his godlike soul wield the government of nature. (Ps. viii.) Yet how defective is that dominion at present! (*Vide* ad. Ps. viii. 7.)

* Heb. i. 5.   † Heb. i. 8.   ‡ Ibid. verse 10.
§ Alexander Gordon's "Design and Use of the Book of Psalms" Phila., 1822. Mr. Gordon was pastor of the Associate Presbyterian congregation, Guinston.

How small is the *manifestation* of that dignity, the *capacity* of which man certainly possesses!—how circumscribed and humbling his present bodily existence!—how much exposed to accident, and how soon destroyed! Hence David says: 'The Lord knoweth our frame: he remembereth that we are dust. As for man, his days are as grass: as a flower of the field, so he flourisheth. For the wind passeth over it and it is gone, and the place thereof shall know it no more.' (Ps. ciii. 14—16.) 'Surely men of low degree are vanity, and men of high degree a lie: to be laid in the balance, they are altogether lighter than vanity.' (Ps. lxii. 9.) And in the eighth Psalm, which celebrates the dignity of man, he exclaims, in contemplation of the infinity and greatness of God in His works: 'What is man, that thou art mindful of him, and the son of man, that thou visitest him?' Thus do the Psalms speak of the impotency and finiteness of man. Thus our perishable condition is by no means the necessary and absolute barrier of created existence, but the effect of internal discord originated by sin. It manifests 'the wrath of God because of sin.' (Cf. Ps. xc. 7—9.) The authors of the Psalms are so alive to a sense of guilt, that the voice of their conscience is audible amid all the accidental trials and sorrows of life, and the mischiefs perpetrated by enemies, and that they acknowledge the justice of the Divine chastisements. (Ad. Ps. xxxviii. 21; cxli. 5.) They feel themselves not entitled to the reception of Divine blessings without the confession of their unworthiness. The exultant spring song of praise in Psalm lxv. is preceded by a confession of sin. They acknowledge that, were God to enter into judgment with man, and to mark his iniquities, none could stand before Him (Ps. cxxx. 3; cxliii. 2; cf. 1 Kings viii. 46; Eccl. vii. 21; Job ix. 2; xiv. 4; xv. 14—16); that unconscious sin, regarded as a condition which apparently contradicts the original of a pure and holy human kind, needs the Divine forgiveness; that sinfulness does not enter into our nature by imitation from without, but that it is in us from the first stages of our existence. (Ps. li. 7.) Far from seeking a ground for justification in our native depravity, David made that confession to indicate the sincerity of his repentance, and to show that he was alive to the full extent of his guilt. What an evidence of the *depth* of the perception of sin is furnished in expressions of pain and grief like those in Psalm xxxii. : 'My bones waxed old through my roaring all the day long; my moisture is turned into the drought of summer'! While natural reason talks only of trespasses against the moral law or man, and on that account remains so cold at the commission of sin, every transgression is regarded in the *Psalms* as a trespass against the Divine Word and the living God, whose will originates the moral law. ' Thy word have I hid in my heart, that I might not sin *against thee*.' (Ps. cxix. 11.) Conscious of his greatest offence against man, he cries, ' Against *thee, thee only*, have I sinned,' rightly apprehending that the most objectionable element of sin is its encroachment upon the Divine law and the proof of man's wilful separation from and opposition to God. Where is to be found a more touching confession of a guilt-convicted conscience than in Psalm xxxii. 3, 4 : ' When I kept silence (intended to conceal), my bones waxed old through my roaring all the day long. For day and night thy hand was heavy upon me : my moisture is turned into the drought of summer' ? The Psalmists occasionally speak of innocence and the purity of their hand (Ps. vii. 9 ; xviii. 21—26; xvii. 3 ; xxvi. 2—6 ; xli. 13); but the preceding observations clearly show that they refer not to absolute integrity before God, but rather to guiltlessness towards *man*. In Psalm xxxviii. the experience of affliction awakes a painful sense of guilt in David, and yet he gives expression to the consciousness of his innocence. He says (Ps. lxix. 4), ' They that hate me without a cause are more than the hairs of mine head' ;

and then adds, 'O God, *thou* knowest my foolishness: and my sins are not hid from *thee*.' (Cf. in Ps. xxv. verses 7, 11, 18, with verses 19—21; and in Ps. xli. verse 5, with verse 13.) The assertion of his purity in Psalm xvii. 3, 4, is preceded by 'Let my sentence come forth from thy presence; let thine eyes behold the things that are equal.' It is incontestably clear from Psalm vii. 3—5, that David refers in verse 8, 'Judge me, O Lord, according to my righteousness and according to mine integrity that is in me,' to righteousness and integrity in relation to specific accusations. And if such were not the case, might not a man, while assuring us of the sincerity of his piety, be at the same time conscious of daily failings and multiform guilt? Such sincerity shows itself when we delight in the commandments of God, and strive to obey them: though the surmounting of obstacles constitutes the business of this life. Who would have expected a confession of sin (Ps. xl. 12) after the description of a heart so completely resigned to the will of God as that which precedes it? The same Asaph who declares God to be his sole consolation and portion was not far from joining in the outrage of the wicked, 'that there is no righteous God in heaven.' (Ps. lxxiii.) How frequently occur expressions like these: 'I will keep thy statutes, I will not forget thy word,' in Psalm cxix.! but that prevents not David from praying, 'Let thy merciful kindness be for my comfort.' (Ps. cxix. 76.) It is to be noticed, that however much the Psalmists refer to their integrity, they never *demand*, but *supplicate* aid and deliverance at the hands of the righteous God; that they hope in that *name* by which the Lord had named himself (Exod. xxxiv. 6), 'Merciful and gracious, long-suffering, and abundant in goodness and truth.' (Psalms xxxi. 4; xl. 12; lxix. 30; cxix. 77; xli. 4; xxv. 11; lii. 11; lxxix. 9; ciii. 8; cxlv. 8.)"*

* Tholuck's Introduc., pp. 37—39.

IV. *The Psalms are full of Christ.* As this is a fact vital to our argument, we enter somewhat into detail; for the Psalms exhibit our Saviour—

(1.) *In his Person, incarnation, and exaltation.* We employ the words of Sommerville: "When the Apostle of the Gentiles would teach the Hebrews the superiority of Christ to all angels—that He is 'God over all, blessed for ever,' the object of worship in heaven and on earth—he appeals almost exclusively to the Book of Psalms. Of seven quotations in the first chapter of the Epistle to the Hebrews, from the Old Testament, six are from the Psalms of David; and some have supposed that the seventh is from the same book. To show the necessary subserviency of the incarnation of Christ to the work of redemption, he refers to the Book of Psalms, in three cases out of four. (Heb. i. ii.) To prove the paramount claim of Messiah, as a prophet and legislator, in comparison with Moses himself, Paul adduces the Psalms. (Heb. iii. iv. 1—13.) When he would show the Divine origin, the dignity, the efficiency, the permanence of the priesthood of Christ, its superiority, in both sacrifice and intercession, to the Aaronic, he turns to the Psalms. (Heb. iv. v.) When he brings forward the doctrine of His ascension to the right hand of the Father, and His investiture with universal authority, he shows that the same is taught in the Book of Psalms." (Rom. xv. 25—28; Heb. ii. 8, 9.)*

(2.) *In all His offices:* "As God-man, He sustains a three-fold office, viz., of a prophet, of a priest, and of a king. As a prophet He teaches the church, and leads his brethren into the knowledge of the name of God. viz., of what God is, what He has done, and what He will in due time perform; and these heads comprehend all that ever has been or will be revealed of the perfections and purposes of God. In the 22d Psalm, He de-

---

* Sommerville on Psalmody, pp. 107, 108, ed. 1858.

clares His purpose and inclination to this great work: 'I will declare thy name unto my brethren; in the midst of the congregation will I praise thee,' verse 22. In the 40th, He speaks of this work as already accomplished: 'I have preached righteousness in the great congregation: lo, I have not refrained my lips, O Lord, thou knowest. I have not hid thy righteousness within my heart; I have declared thy faithfulness and thy salvation: I have not concealed thy loving-kindness and thy truth from the great congregation,' verses 9, 10. It is evident that the same person speaks in the verses immediately before who speaks in these; and all may be satisfied that it is Christ who speaks, by reading the 5th to the 9th verses inclusive of the 10th chapter of the Hebrews.

"Of His priesthood we have a most particular account in the 110th Psalm: 'The Lord hath sworn, and will not repent, Thou art a *priest* for ever, after the order of Melchizedek,' verse 4. In the 40th, we find Him entering on the discharge of this office: 'Lo, I come: in the volume of the book it is written of me. To do thy will, O my God, I take delight; yea, thy law is within my heart,' ver. 7, 8. In contemplation of His combat with the powers of darkness, and His endurance of the punishment of the sins which He had taken upon Himself, He prays in the remainder of the Psalm for Divine assistance. And while engaged in presenting His one offering, through the Eternal Spirit, without spot unto God, his thoughts and feelings are expressed in a most moving manner, in the 22d; and in the 31st we have the very words with which He poured out His soul unto death: 'Into thy hand I commit my spirit,' verse 5.

"His anointing set Him apart also to the office of King of the church, and Head over all things. In the 2d Psalm this is particularly mentioned: 'Yet have I set my King upon my holy hill of Zion,' verse 6. In the 45th and 89th, we find the perpetuity of His throne and kingdom: 'Thy throne, O God, is for ever and ever'; 'His seed and throne shall endure as the days of heaven.' In the same 45th, and also in the 72d, we have the nature of His government described: 'The sceptre of thy kingdom is a right sceptre'; 'He shall judge the people with righteousness, and the poor with equity.' In the 16th, His resurrection from the dead is celebrated; in which He arose as a mighty conqueror over death and him that hath the power of it: 'Thou wilt not leave my soul in hell, nor suffer thy Holy One to see corruption,' verse 10. (Acts ii. 27—31.) His triumphant ascent into the third heavens, we have already seen, is celebrated in the 47th; 'God is gone up with a shout, the Lord with the sound of a trumpet'; and in the 68th, 'Thou hast ascended up on high; thou hast led captivity captive; thou hast received gifts for men.' The triumph with which He was received into paradise is expressed in the 24th: 'Lift up your heads, O ye gates; even lift them up, ye everlasting doors; and the *King* of glory shall come in. Who is this King of glory? The Lord of hosts, he is the King of glory,' verses 9, 10. In the 110th, the Psalmist speaks of His inauguration: 'The Lord said unto my Lord, Sit thou at my right hand until I make thine enemies thy footstool,' verse 1. (Heb. x. 12, 13.) The universal authority which He will exercise till the period come when His wrath shall kindle against His enemies, and burn to the lowest hell, is described in the 2d and 8th, which last compare with Heb. ii. 6, 7, 8."*

(3.) *In His tenderness and compassion, His fidelity and constancy.* He is the "Shepherd," compassionate and bountiful (Ps. cxxiii., lxxx); the almighty and vigilant Guardian (Ps. cxxi.); the faithful and gracious Rewarder (Ps. xviii.); more faithful and constant than father or mother (Ps. xxvii.); the sure portion of the believer, and of the redeemed and glorified. (Ps. xvi., lxxiii., cxix.)

* Gordon, pp. 38—41.

(4.) *In the extensive triumphs of His Gospel and kingdom.* Thus, when the apostle Paul would trace the setting up of a ministry, &c., in the church, for the "edifying of the body of Christ," he quotes (chap. 18) from the Book of Psalms. When he would confirm the right of the Gentiles to the Gospel and its privileges, he again resorts to the Book of Psalms: " Now I say that Jesus Christ was a minister of the circumcision for the truth of God, to confirm the promises made unto the fathers ; and that the Gentiles might glorify God for his mercy," as it is written : " For this cause, I will confess to thee among the Gentiles, and sing unto thy name. And again, praise the Lord all ye Gentiles, and laud him all ye people." (Rom. xv. 8, 9, 11.)*

No less clearly do the Psalms exhibit " the subjugation of His enemies, implying the confounding of Satan's policy, and the destruction of his kingdom, with all those interests that hang upon it, viz., Pagan idolatry, Popish superstition, and Mahomedan delusion ; and the extension of His kingdom, which implies the diffusion of Gospel knowledge by the various means of grace ; the conversion of the Jews and the Gentile nations to the true religion. (To accomplish all this, we have reason to expect an abundant outpouring of the Holy Spirit.) An outline of all these great events we have beautifully foretold in the 72d. It applies, indeed, to Solomon and his kingdom as types ; but it applies truly and properly to Christ and His kingdom : ' He shall judge thy people with righteousness, and thy poor with judgment. He shall judge the poor of thy people ; he shall save the children of the needy, and shall break in pieces the oppressor.' Such is the character of His administration. ' He shall come down like rain upon the mown grass, and as showers that water the earth': such the abundant influence of

---

* Sommerville, p. 109.

His Holy Spirit. 'He shall have dominion also from sea to sea, and from the river unto the ends of the earth. They that dwell in the wilderness shall bow before him. The kings of Tarshish and the isles shall bring presents: the kings of Sheba and Seba shall offer gifts. Yea, *all kings* shall fall down before him; all nations shall serve him. And He shall live, and to *Him* shall be given of the gold of Sheba': such shall be the extent and prosperity of His kingdom. 'There shall be an handful of corn in the earth, on the top of the mountains; the fruit thereof shall shake like Lebanon, and they of the city shall flourish like grass of the earth.' Such will be the glorious success of the everlasting Gospel, by which the immortal seed of the Word shall be sown, until 'all nations shall call him blessed,' and 'the whole earth shall be filled with his glory'; which is the highest and last wish of David the son of Jesse, and of all true Christians."*

(5.) *Even in most of the leading particulars of His life.* The following have been selected by Sommerville: "1st. The rejection of Christ by the Jewish doctors. 'The stone which the builders rejected is become the head of the corner. This is the Lord's doing; it is marvellous in our eyes.' The application of these words is made by Jesus himself, and twice by Peter. Compare Matt. xxi. 42, Acts iv. 11, 1 Peter ii. 7—8, with Psalms cxviii. 22—23.

"2d. The circumstances of His public entrance into Jerusalem are declared in the spirit of prophecy. 'Out of the mouth of babes and sucklings thou hast ordained strength, because of thine enemies, that thou mightest still the enemy and the avenger.' The Saviour points out the application of these words. He enters Jerusalem seated on an ass, attended by a multitude, some spreading their garments in the way, some strew-

---

* Gordon, pp. 48—49.

ing branches, all proclaiming, ' Hosanna to the Son of David: blessed is He that cometh in the name of the Lord: hosanna in the highest'; and He displays His authority as a son over His own house by turning those out of the temple who had converted His Father's residence into a place of merchan'dise. ' And when the chief priests and scribes saw the wonderful things that he did, and the children crying in the temple, and saying, Hosanna to the Son of David, they were sore displeased, and said unto him, Hearest thou what they say? And Jesus saith unto them, Yea, have ye never read, Out of the mouth of babes and sucklings thou hast perfected praise?' The priests and scribes are silent. The enemy and avenger is stilled. Compare Ps. viii. 2, with Matt. xxi. 5—16.

" 3d. In the Psalms the combination of all nations against the Saviour is revealed: ' The kings of the earth set themselves, and the rulers take counsel together, against the Lord, and against his anointed, saying, Let us break their bands asunder and cast away their cords from us.' And we learn the views of the disciples respecting the passage from the following words: ' For of a truth against thy holy child Jesus, whom thou hast anointed, both Herod and Pontius Pilate, with the Gentiles and the people of Israel, were gathered together, for to do whatsoever thy hand and thy counsel determined before to be done.' Ps. ii. 2, 3, compared with Acts iv. 26—28.

" 4th. The partition of Christ's raiment, when He is being crucified, with the particular mode by which His seamless coat was disposed of, is set before us in the Book of Psalms: ' They part my garment among them, and cast lots upon my vesture.' How literally was this verified in the Man of Nazareth! So literal was the accomplishment that no man can doubt that Messiah speaks in the 22d Psalm, by the mouth of David. As the words of the Son of David it was received by the Evangelist: ' Then the soldiers, when they had crucified Jesus, took his garments, and made four parts, to every soldier a part; and also his coat: now the coat was without seam, woven from the top throughout. They said, therefore, among themselves, Let us not rend it, but cast lots for it, whose it shall be: that the Scripture might be fulfilled, which saith, They parted my raiment among them, and for my vesture they did cast lots.' (John xix. 23, 24.)

" 5th. The Jews read and sang in the Psalms the Saviour's pathetic expression of His sense of desertion, in the hour when the powers of darkness were let loose, and His expression of confidential reliance when about to give up the ghost: ' My God, my God, why hast thou forsaken me?' 'Into thine hand I commit my spirit.' Ps. xxii. 1, and xxxi. 5, compared with Matt. xxvii. 46, and Luke xxiii. 46."*

In all this detail, we have but furnished some examples for the purpose of showing how comprehensive is the view presented by this inspired manual of the person, offices, works, life, and triumphs of the Church's Redeemer and King: enough to satisfy the considerate and candid, that we need not to sing of Christ, and celebrate His work of mediation, pass beyond its limits.

V. *The Psalms contain the richest fund of Christian experience.* They abound, as we have already seen, in acknowledgments of the felt insignificancy of man. There are to be found in them heart-broken confessions of sin in its guilt, defilement, and power (Ps. li., xix., xxxii., cxxx., &c.); most earnest supplications for pardon (Ps. xxx., &c); these prayers addressed to God as a merciful God, and in dependence upon the " blood of sprinkling" (Ps. li., xxxi., &c.); a deep and abiding sense of the absolute need of Divine teaching, and of the help of the Spirit of Christ (Ps. xxx., li., cxxxix.); ardent spiritual desires and affections (Ps. xliii., xliv.,

---

* Sommerville, pp. 109—112.

lxiii., lxxiii., cxix.) ; strong faith, sometimes conflicting with remaining unbelief (Ps. iii., iv., &c.) ; gratitude and thanksgiving on almost every page : hopes of heavenly blessedness (Ps. xvi., lxxiii.); deep interest in the welfare of the church, of friends, of brethren, of mankind (Ps. cxxii., xxxv., xcv., xcvi., cxix., &c.); the duty and the happy results of true Christian unity (Ps. cxxii., cxxxiii.); happy anticipations of the church's millennial glory and peace, extension, and prosperity (Ps. lxxii., xcvi., &c.) ; adoring praise everywhere throughout the Psalms, rising to the loftiest strains (Ps. cxlix., cl.) ; high esteem of the Word of God, and devout recognition of His law, in its extent, purity, spirituality, and obligation. (Ps. xix., xxv., cxix.)

Such is the Book of Psalms, and more than this. Such, too, has been the estimate ever put upon it by the most eminent Christians and Christian teachers, ancient and modern. We furnish some of their sayings. Chrysostom says : " The grace of the Holy Ghost hath so ordered it, that the Psalms of David should be recited and sung night and day. In the church's vigils—in the morning—at funeral solemnities —the first, the midst, and the last is David. In private houses, where virgins spin — in the monasteries—in the deserts, where men converse with God— the first, the midst, and the last is David. In the night, when men sleep, he wakes them up to sing; and collecting the servants of God into angelic troops, turns earth into heaven, and of men makes angels, chanting David's Psalms." Athanasius, bishop of Alexandria, in the fourth century, says : " They appear to me a mirror of the soul of every one who sings them; they enable him to perceive his own emotions, and to express them in the words of the Psalms. He who hears them read receives them as if they were spoken for him. Conscience-struck, he will either humbly repent, or hearing how the trust of believers was rewarded by God, rejoice as if His mercy were promised to him in particular, and begin to thank God. Yes, in its pages you find pourtrayed man's whole life, the emotion of his soul and the frames of his mind. We cannot conceive of anything richer than the Book of Psalms. If you need penitence, if anguish or temptation have befallen you, if you have escaped persecution and oppression, or are immersed in deep affliction, concerning each and all you may find instruction, and state it to God in the words of the Psalter!" Let us add Ambrose, the pious bishop of Milan, in the fourth century:—" The law instructs, history informs, prophecy predicts, correction censures, and morals exhort. In the Book of Psalms you find the fruit of all these, as well as a remedy for the salvation of the soul. The Psalter deserves to be called the praise of God, the glory of man, the voice of the church, and the most beneficial confession of faith. The Psalms teach me to avoid sin, and to *unlearn* my being *ashamed* of repentance. In the Psalms delight and instruction vie with one another: we sing for enjoyment and read for instruction." Augustine relates with deep feeling, in his Confessions, what a treasure the Psalms were to him at the time of his conversion. " How did I then," says he in addressing God, " converse with thee, when I read the Psalms of David—those songs full of faith, those accents which exclude all pride! How did I address thee in those Psalms!—how did they kindle my love to thee!—how did they animate me, if possible, to read them out to the whole world, as a protest against the pride of the human race! And yet they *are* sung in the whole world; ' nothing is hid from their heat.'* How violent was my indignation against the Manichæans (the heretical sect who entirely rejected the Old Testament), and yet felt pity for their not knowing those holy riches, those remedies, and their raging against the antidote that might have healed them! I

---

* A beautiful allusion to Psalm xix. 7.

wish they had been at my side—yet without my knowledge—beheld my countenance and heard my voice when I read the fourth Psalm: what a blessing it was to me! O that they could have heard, but without my knowledge of their being within hearing (lest they should fancy I was speaking for their sakes), what I said to thee at the occasion of those words!" He then states, with profound emotion, what passed in his soul at the reading of every separate verse of that Psalm.

The words of Luther's pregnant Preface to the Psalter are well known. We make from it the following extract: "The human heart is like a vessel in a tempestuous sea, tossed to and fro by the storms from the four quarters of the world. Fear and care of future mishap are roaring here; grief and sadness on account of present evil there. Hope and courage respecting future happiness are blowing here, while assurance and joy on account of present good are sounding there. Such tempests teach one to be in earnest, now to open and now to pour out one's heart. He who is in fear and trouble talks in other strains about mishap than he who lives in joy; and he who lives in joy in other strains than he who lives in fear. It comes not from the heart (they say) when a sad one tries to laugh and a glad one to weep: *i.e.*, his heart is neither opened nor poured out. But what do you find most in the Psalms? Earnest speech in all manner of tempests. Where can you find more appropriate expressions of joy than in the Psalms of praise and thanksgiving? You look right into the hearts of saints, as into fair and pleasant gardens, or heaven itself, and behold beautiful, laughing, and delicate flowers of all manner of fair and joyous thoughts towards God and His love springing lustily into life. Again: where can you find more profound, plaintive, and wretched words of grief than in the Psalms of complaint? Once more you look into the heart of saints as into death or hell. How gloomy and dark their mournful visions of God! So, again, when the Psalms speak of fear and hope, they abound in words so significant that no painter could thus pourtray, no Cicero nor orator thus describe them."

Let us now hear Calvin. In the Preface of his Exposition of the Psalms, he mentions with holy earnestness the blessing he himself had derived from being engaged in that work, and the aid with which his own experience, both temporal and spiritual, furnished him in the Exposition of the Psalms of the Bible. But let him speak for himself: "If the reading of my Commentaries yield to the church of God as much blessing as their preparation has conferred upon me, I shall never repent having undertaken the task." "Not without good grounds am I wont to call this book an anatomy of all parts of the soul, since no one can experience emotions whose portrait he could not behold reflected in its mirror. Yes, the Holy Spirit has there depicted in the most vivid manner every species of pain, affliction, fear, doubt, hope, care, anxiety, and turbulent emotion, through which the hearts of men are chased. Other portions of the Scriptures contain commandments whose transmission the Lord enjoined upon his servants; but in the Psalms, the prophets, communing with God and uncovering their inmost feelings, call and urge every reader to self-examination to such a degree, that of the numerous infirmities to which we are liable, and of the many failings which oppress us, not one remains concealed. How great and rare, again, for the human heart to be thus driven out of all its hiding-places, liberated from hypocrisy (that most fearful of vices), and exposed to the light! Lastly, if calling on God is the surest means of our salvation—if better and more reliable directions for it than those contained in the Book of Psalms are not to be obtained—then every one who reads this book has attained to an essential part of the Divine doctrine. Earnest prayer originates in our sense of need; afterwards in our faith in the Divine promises. The reader of the Psalms finds himself both aroused to feel his misery and exhorted to seek for its remedy. You cannot read anywhere more glorious praises of God's peculiar grace towards His church or of His works; you cannot find anywhere such an enumeration of man's deliverances or praises for the glorious proofs of His fatherly care for us, or a more perfect representation to praise Him becomingly, or more fervent exhortations to the discharge of that holy duty. But, however rich the book may prove in all these respects to fit us for a holy, pious, and just life, its *chief* lesson is, how we are to *bear the cross*, and to give the true evidence of our obedience, by parting with our affections, to submit ourselves to God, to suffer our lives to be entirely guided by His will, so that the bitterest trial, because He sends it, seems sweet to us. Finally, not only is the goodness of God praised in general terms to secure our perfect resignation to Him, and to expect His aid in every time of need, but the free forgiveness of our sins, which alone can effect our *peace of conscience* and reconciliation to God, are in particular so strongly recommended, that there is nothing wanting to the knowledge of eternal life."*

Tholuck himself says: "Who can remain untouched on hearing the words of David at the beginning of the psalm of thanksgiving which he sung towards the close of his life, and which may be regarded as the result of his experience of life—'I will love thee, O Lord, my strength'? (Psalm xviii. 1.) 'Thou art my Lord, all my goods I prefer not to thee.' (Psalm xvi. 2.) 'This I know, for *God is for me.*' No Christian could describe in sweeter language the peace of reconciliation than we find it done in Psalms xvi., xxiii., ciii., lxxiii., xxvi., xxvii., lxxi., 14—24, &c. How happy must have been their communion with God who say, 'How excellent is thy loving-kindness, O God! therefore the children of men put their trust under the shadow of thy wings:

* Tholuck's Comm., pp. 5—9.

they are abundantly satisfied with the fatness of thy house, and thou makest them drink of the river of thy pleasures.' (Psalm xxxvi. 8, 9.) 'Blessed is the man whom thou choosest and causest to approach unto thee, that he may dwell in thy courts; we shall be satisfied with the goodness of thy house, even of thy holy temple.' (Psalm lxv. 5.) 'Thy loving-kindness is better than life, when I remember thee upon my bed, and meditate on thee in the night watches.' (Psalm lxiii. 4, 7.)"* We add the well-known testimony of the eminent Edwards: "The oil that was used in anointing David was a type of the Spirit of God; and the type and the antitype were given both together, as we are told, 1 Sam. xvi. 13: 'Then the Spirit of the Lord came upon David from that day forward.' One way that His Spirit influenced him was by inspiring him to show forth Christ and the glorious things of His redemption in divine songs, sweetly expressing the breathings of a pious soul, full of the admiration of the glorious things of the Redeemer, inflamed with divine love and elevated praise; and therefore he is called the sweet Psalmist of Israel, 2 Sam. xxiii. 1. The main subjects of these songs were the glorious things of the Gospel, as is evident by the interpretation that is often put upon them, and the use that is made of them in the New Testament; for there is no one book of the Old Testament that is so often quoted in the New as the Book of Psalms. Joyfully did this holy man sing of those great things of Christ's redemption that had been the hope and expectation of God's church and people from the beginning; and joyfully did others follow him in it, as Asaph, Heman, and others. Here Christ is spoken of in multitudes of songs, speaking of His incarnation, life, death, resurrection, ascension into heaven; His satisfaction, intercession; His prophetical, kingly, and priestly office; His glorious benefits in this life and that which is to come; His union with the church,

* Ibid, pp. 39—40.

and the blessedness of the church in Him ; His calling of the Gentiles ; the future glory of the church near the end of the world, and Christ's coming to the final judgment. All these things, and many more concerning Christ and His redemption, are abundantly spoken of in the Book of Psalms."

"This was a glorious advancement of the affair of redemption, as God hereby gave His church a book of divine songs for their use in that part of their public worship, namely, singing His praise throughout *all ages to the end of the world*. It is manifest *the Book of Psalms was given of God for this end*. It was used in the church of Israel *by God's appointment*. And we find that *the same* are appointed in the New Testament to be made use of in the Christian church, in their worship: Eph. v. 19; Col. iii. 16—in psalms, hymns, and *spiritual songs*. So they have been, and will, *to the end of the world*, be made use of in the church to celebrate the praises of God." "The Psalms of David were penned for the use of the Church of God in its public worship, not only in that age, but in other ages, as being fitted to express the religion of all saints, in all ages, as well as the religion of the Psalmist."

"They present religion to us," says Bishop Horne, "in its most engaging dress; communicating truths which philosophy could never investigate, in a style which poetry can never equal; while history is made the vehicle of prophecy, and creation lends all its charms to paint the glories of redemption."

What more does the Church require? In these Psalms of the Bible, we may celebrate the glorious perfections of our God, and His righteous and benevolent dominion over the earth and the heavens: we may express our most humble and evangelical convictions of insignificancy and unworthiness, in contrast with the ineffable majesty, the immaculate purity, the infinite righteousness of Jehovah ; we may contemplate in these inspired songs, and magnify, the person, work, grace, and fulness of Jesus Christ; we are here furnished with language in which to express the most lowly, as also the most enlarged and elevated gracious affections; we are here provided with prayers and arguments to enforce our petitions, suited to every emergency and every trial: as we sing these psalms, we may anticipate with sure hope the future deliverances, triumphs, prosperity, and universal extension of the Church of Christ on earth, with the entire subjugation or utter ruin of her enemies and His; and thus foresee with joy and praise the glorious issue of the dispensation of mercy, in the ultimate establishment of the mediatorial dominion to the ends of the earth, reaching forth to the final judgment, and to the unseen glories of the heavenly state and the everlasting blessedness of God's redeemed.

Why, then, any other book of psalms or hymns? And should not the very fact, that such a book, so complete and perfect, has been given to the Church, go far to satisfy us that no other manual of praise was ever to supersede this—that none can take its place, or, with God's approbation, come in competition with it?

CHAPTER II.

THE BOOK OF PSALMS HAS THE SEAL OF DIVINE APPOINTMENT, WHICH NONE OTHER HAS.

I. *These Psalms have the seal of Divine appointment.* We give the argument, and the history of the ordinance of praise in the words of Dr. Pressly:—"If it can be made to appear to the satisfaction of the reader, that the songs contained in the Book of Psalms were given to the church to be used in celebrating the praise of God, it will then be admitted that the point in dispute is settled; for with all who receive the Bible as the rule of faith, it is a received principle, that in the worship of God, divine appointment is our guide. What evidence, then, have we, that the psalms and hymns and songs contained in the Book of Psalms, were appointed by God, to be used in the celebration of His praise?

"The Divine inspiration of the Book of Psalms will be admitted by all who are interested in the present discussion. Though it must be confessed that language is sometimes employed by those who plead for the use of hymns, in relation to those Divine songs contained in the Book of Psalms, which is utterly inconsistent with the reverence which is due to the word of God, and which would seem to indicate, that in reality they are regarded as the productions of mere human genius. They who denominate some of these sacred hymns, 'cursing psalms,' and represent the Psalmist as giving vent to feelings of malevolence towards his personal enemies, surely do not regard him as one by whose mouth the Holy Ghost spake. But however incautiously and irreverently some men may have spoken of these Divine songs, yet all who believe in the inspiration of the Scriptures, will admit that the Book of Psalms is the word of God, and is, in common with other parts of the Bible, the rule of faith and practice. But while the Book of Psalms is a revelation from God, and is, in common with the rest of the lively oracles, profitable for instruction in righteousness, it is profitable, especially as containing matter adapted to a particular purpose. In this book, the high praises of our God are celebrated by the Divine Spirit, who 'searcheth all things; yea, the deep things of God;' and, therefore, these songs are profitable to the church, especially for the purpose of praising God, which is an end to which some other parts of Divine revelation are not adapted. Everything contained in the sacred volume is useful to the church of God; but some portions of the word of revelation are more appropriate to one purpose, while others are more especially adapted to another. And the Book of Psalms is adapted to the edification of the church of God, especially as furnishing matter suitable to be employed in singing God's praise. That these songs were given to the church to be sung in the worship of God, is evident from the peculiar character of their matter; the titles by which the Holy Ghost designates them; and from the use which was originally made of them by the church of God.

"The matter of these Divine songs is peculiar, and indicates the particular end for which they were intended. Here* the glory of Jehovah is celebrated in the sublimest strains of Eastern poetry, as displayed in the works of creation and of redemption; and the church is furnished with suitable matter for praising God for His goodness, wisdom, power, love, and mercy, manifested in the salvation of man, the preservation of the church, and the government of the world. As then, the peculiar character of the contents of any composition manifests the end for which it was intended; as from its matter, we know that one composition is a political essay; another is a philosophical speculation; and a third, is a biographical sketch of some distinguished individual; so, from the matter of the Book of Psalms, we learn that its peculiar design is the celebration of God's praise, and that it was given to the church to be employed peculiarly for that purpose. 'Praise ye the Lord; for it is good to sing praises to our God; for it is pleasant, and praise is comely.' These Divine songs abound with ascriptions of praise to God, and with urgent calls, addressed not only to the church in her collective capacity, but to all classes of men, to engage in this delightful exercise: 'Praise the Lord, O Jerusalem! praise thy God, O Zion!' 'Let every thing that hath breath praise the Lord.'

* See Cap. I.

"The titles which the Holy Spirit has employed to designate these divine hymns indicate the particular use for which they were intended. The reader will please to remember what has been said in a preceding chapter on the words of the Apostle, when he exhorts the church to engage in the duty of singing 'psalms and hymns and spiritual songs.' It is believed that no interpretation of the Apostle's language can be sustained which does not proceed upon the principle, that there is a reference to the different songs contained in the Book of Psalms. And this being admitted, it will follow that we have an explicit Divine direction to employ these songs in the worship of God. But, independent of this consideration, it is undeniable that the Holy Spirit appropriates to this collection of sacred songs—the title, 'the Book of Psalms,' or songs of praise. By this title they are referred to repeatedly in the New Testament. For example, our Lord, when speaking with reference to this portion of Divine revelation, says, 'David himself saith in the Book of Psalms.' (Luke xx. 42.) And in accordance with this is the language of the Apostle Peter: 'It is written in the Book of Psalms.' (Acts i. 20) The word 'Psalm' is of Greek derivation, and comes from a word which signifies to sing. Psalms, then, are songs which are to be sung. And, by giving to this collection of sacred songs, the title of the Book of Psalms, the Holy Spirit recognised them as songs of praise to be sung in the worship of God. That these songs were originally used by the church in singing the praise of God, is a matter of historical record.

"Since, then, the Book of Psalms is a collection of songs given to the church by the Holy Spirit, the matter of which indicates that their peculiar design is to set forth the praise of God; since, the Holy Spirit has designated this collection, 'the Book of Psalms,' or a book of songs of praise; since, they are denominated 'the Songs of Zion,' and 'the Songs of the Lord;'

and since, we learn from the sacred Scriptures, that these songs were used by the church of God, with Divine approbation; therefore, we conclude, that these songs were given to the church by her glorious King, to be employed in singing God's praise.

"That the force of the argument in favour of the Divine appointment of the Book of Psalms to be employed in the worship of God may more clearly appear, it may be of advantage, in this connexion, to review briefly the history of this part of religious worship, as it may be deduced from the Sacred Scriptures.

"In the primitive ages of the world, the worship of the Deity, it would appear, consisted chiefly in prayer, in connexion with the offering of sacrifice. There is no evidence furnished by anything contained in the Sacred History that the singing of God's praise formed any part of the regular worship of God. The first example recorded in the Bible in which the people of God are represented as engaged in a social capacity in this exercise of religious worship, is on the occasion of that signal display of the Divine power and goodness manifested in the deliverance of Israel at the Red Sea, while their Egyptian adversaries experienced a terrible overthrow:—'Then sang Moses and the children of Israel this song unto the Lord, and spake, saying, I will sing unto the Lord, for he hath triumphed gloriously; the horse and his rider hath he thrown into the sea.' On a subsequent occasion, Deborah, a prophetess, furnished a song commemorative of the Divine goodness in delivering Israel from the yoke of Jabin, the king of Canaan: 'Then sang Deborah and Barak, the son of Abinoam, on that day, saying, Praise the Lord for the avenging of Israel.' At that time, there had not yet been provided a Book of Psalms, containing a collection of songs adapted to the diversified circumstances of God's people; nor have we any evidence that the singing of God's praise constituted any part of the stated worship of Jehovah; but when the circumstances of Divine Providence called for a public expression of gratitude to God, some individual was raised up, who, under the direction of the Spirit of God, furnished a song suited to the occasion.

"At least as early as the days of Samuel, there were established in the Hebrew commonwealth schools of the prophets. These seminaries of sacred learning were under the superintendence of some distinguished prophet, and in them the youth destined to the prophetic office were employed in the study of Divine things. Though the Sacred History has given us but little information relative to the exercises in which the youth in these schools were employed, we learn that one particular part of their business was the celebration of God's praise in sacred songs, accompanied by instruments of music. Saul, as Samuel had foretold, when he came to the hill of God, which was the seat of one of these colleges, was met by a company of prophets, who '*prophesied upon the psaltery, and tabret, and pipe, and harp*'; and, seized by a Divine impulse, Saul joined the company, and prophesied also. And on a subsequent occasion, when Saul sent messengers to Naioth to apprehend David, we are told that when the messengers saw the company of prophets prophesying, and Samuel standing as appointed over them, the Spirit of God was upon the messengers of Saul, and they also prophesied. By prophesying, in these examples, is evidently meant the celebration of God's praise, in sacred songs, under a Divine influence. Accordingly, the sons of Asaph and Jeduthun, musicians in the temple, are represented as prophesying with a harp, to give thanks, and to praise the Lord.

"In these sacred colleges established in Israel, then, it appears that, among other employments, poetry and music were cultivated by the sons of the prophets. Sacred hymns were composed under a Divine influence, and were sung in the worship of God, accompanied by musical instruments. Whether any of the hymns composed in these schools of the prophets have been transmitted to us, in that collection of sacred songs denominated the Book of Psalms, we have not the means of determining with certainty.

"At length, however, in the person of David, a prophet was raised up, whom the Spirit of the Lord eminently qualified for this purpose—who not only composed a great variety of sacred hymns, but also reduced the public worship of God into a regular system, of which the singing of praise formed a part. That David was divinely qualified for this service, and called to it, is sufficiently evident from the express language of the Bible:—' Now these be the last words of David: David, the son of Jesse, said, and the man who was raised up on high, the anointed of the God of Jacob, and the sweet psalmist of Israel, said, The Spirit of the Lord spake by me, and his word was in my tongue.' (2 Sam. xxiii. 1, 2.) In the worship of the ancient tabernacle, according to the appointment of Moses, the Israelites were directed to express their joy in God by blowing with trumpets at the time of offering the sacrifices:—' In the day of your gladness, and in your solemn days, and in the beginnings of your months, ye shall blow with the trumpets over your burnt-offerings, and over the sacrifices of your peace-offerings.' (Numb. x. 10.) But in connexion with the offering of sacrifice, David introduced the singing of praise. By his direction the Levites were numbered and distributed into classes, that among other services connected with the worship of the temple they might 'stand every morning to thank and to praise the Lord, and likewise at evening.' (1 Chron. xxiii. 30.) And in the performance of this part of their service the custom was, that when the offering was presented on the altar, the Levites began to sing the praise of God:—' When the burnt-offering began, the song of the Lord began also, with the trumpets and with the instruments ordained by David, king of Israel.' (2 Chron. xxix. 27.) And that these regulations in the worship of God and in the services of the temple were made, not by his own private authority, but by Divine direction, we have sufficient evidence.

"In the instructions which David gave to Solomon with regard to the temple and its worship, according to 'the pattern of all that he had by the Spirit,' there are included directions for the priests and the Levites, and for all the work of the service of the house of the Lord. And in relation to these instructions generally, it is added—'All this the Lord made me understand in writing by his hand upon me, even all the works of this pattern.' (1 Chron. xxviii. 13—19.) And as a further confirmation of the conclusion that, in all these regulations connected with the worship of God, David was directed by Divine wisdom, it is stated in the history of the reformation effected under the reign of Hezekiah, that this pious king 'set the Levites in the house of the Lord, with cymbals, with psalteries, and with harps, according to the commandment of David, and of Gad, the king's seer, and Nathan, the prophet; for so was the commandment of the Lord by his prophets.' (2 Chron. xxix. 25.)

"From this historical survey, then, it appears that we have no evidence that, previous to the age of David, the singing of God's praise formed a part of the stated worship of God. But on particular occasions, when the dispensations of Divine Providence towards the church called for a public expression of their gratitude, the people of God poured forth their thankful acknowledgments in songs of praise ; and at such times some one who was divinely qualified, by being filled with the Holy Ghost, furnished a hymn suited to the exigencies of the church. But in all the history of the church, as recorded in the Bible, there is no evidence whatever that any person presumed to undertake such a service who was not divinely called to it, by being endowed with the spirit of inspiration.

"At length, after the Lord God of Israel had given rest unto His people, and they were in quiet possession of the land promised to their fathers, God raised up, in the person of David, a prophet, by whom the public worship of God was reduced into a regular system, of which the singing of praise formed a part. And as the celebration of God's praise now became a regular part of divine worship, it became indispensably necessary that divine songs should be provided for the use of the church. Accordingly, God, who selects His own instruments for the accomplishment of His work, called David to the performance of this most important service. By the inspiration of the Holy Spirit he was endowed with those peculiar gifts which were necessary to qualify him for the office of 'a sweet psalmist of Israel;' and by his instrumentality the church was furnished with a choice variety of 'psalms, hymns, and spiritual songs,' adapted to the diversified circumstances of the private believer and of the church of God. 'In these songs,' as the celebrated Edwards very justly observes, 'David speaks of the incarnation, life, death, resurrection, ascension into heaven, satisfaction and intercession of Christ; His prophetical, kingly, and priestly office; His glorious benefits in this life and that which is to come; His union with the church; the blessedness of the church in Him; the calling of the Gentiles; the future glory of the church, near the end of the world; and the coming of Christ to the final judgment.'* The singing of praise to God, from this time forth, formed a part of the regular worship of God, and by the sweet Psalmist of Israel, the anointed of the God of Jacob, by whom the Spirit of the Lord spake, the Church of God was furnished with songs to be employed in divine worship.

"The divine appointment of these songs to be used in the worship of God, is just as conclusively established, as that David was raised up on high, the anointed of the God of Jacob, and the sweet Psalmist of Israel, by

* History of Redemption.

whom the Spirit of the Lord spake. And accordingly, as a matter of historical record, we know that these songs were used by the church with divine approbation. At the dedication of the temple, it appears that among others, the 136th Psalm was sung. The Levites praised the Lord, saying, 'For he is good, for his mercy endureth for ever.' And in testimony of the divine approbation, 'The house was filled with a cloud, even the house of the Lord, so that the priests could not minister by reason of the cloud; for the glory of the Lord had filled the house of God.' (2 Chron. xv. 13, 14.) And in the history of the reformation which took place during the reign of Hezekiah, who did that which was right in the sight of the Lord, according to all that David his father had done, we are informed that 'Hezekiah the king, and the princes, commanded the Levites to sing praise unto the Lord, with the words of David and Asaph the seer.' (2 Chron. xxix. 30.) David, who by way of eminence was styled the sweet Psalmist of Israel, was the principal individual employed in furnishing songs of praise for the use of the church; but Asaph, Heman, Jeduthun, and others, performed their part in the same interesting service. These holy men of God, who were endowed with the requisite gifts by the Spirit of inspiration, furnished for the use of the church, that rich and varied collection of divine hymns contained in the Book of Psalms.

"By whom these songs, which were evidently composed by different persons, and on a great variety of occasions, were collected into a book and arranged in their present order, we are not able to determine with absolute certainty. There is, however, strong probability in support of the conclusion that this service was performed by Ezra. This distinguished priest and scribe, who acted a conspicuous part in that reformation which was effected in connexion with the return of the Jews from Babylon, according to Jewish tradition, by Divine direction, collected and arranged the different portions of the sacred writings then extant, and digested them in that systematic order in which they have been handed down to us. But let this matter be decided as it may, it is sufficient for us to know, that whoever may have collected these songs together, it was done with Divine approbation ; for the writers of the New Testament refer to them by the title, 'The Book of Psalms.' And to use the language of the celebrated writer already referred to, 'it is manifest that the Book of Psalms was given of God for this end ;' that is, that it might be used by the church in singing God's praise. 'It was used in the church of Israel by God's appointment. This is manifest by the title of many of the psalms, in which they are inscribed to the chief musician; that is, to the man that was appointed to be the leader of divine songs in the temple, in the public worship of Israel.'

"In this conclusion, then, we rest. In the revelation which God has given to His church, we find a collection of divine songs, the matter of which, the titles by which they are designated, and the use which was originally made of them with divine approbation, manifest that the specific end for which they were given, was, that they should be employed in singing God's praise ; and being communicated to the church by her God and King, for this purpose, they should be used in this part of divine worship.*

II. *Such appointment can be claimed for no other songs or manual of praise.* "There is no Book of Psalms in the New Testament. The duty of singing God's praise is very distinctly recognised in the New Testament. 'By him,' says the Apostle to the Hebrews, 'let us offer the sacrifice of praise to God continually, that is, the fruit of our lips, giving thanks to his name.' (Heb. xiii. 15.) And again : 'Is any merry ? Let him sing psalms.' (James v. 13.) At the close of the last

Pressly on Psalmody, pp. 70.-81.

passover, our Lord and His disciples sung a hymn. And in the gloomy precincts of a dungeon, Paul and Silas, at the hour of midnight, 'prayed and sang praises unto God.' 'But, while we are exhorted to offer unto God the sacrifice of praise, and have the example of our Lord and of His Apostles to excite us to engage in this delightful exercise, we find no collection of psalms, and hymns, and songs, in the New Testament. In what sense is it reasonable to suppose, that the primitive Christians would understand the apostolic direction, 'Is any merry? Let him sing psalms.' To assist the plain Christian in determining what is the proper answer to this inquiry, let me propose another question. When our Lord said to his hearers, 'Search the Scriptures;' in what sense is it to be supposed, that this direction would be understood? No one will pretend that our Lord designed that His hearers should understand Him as instructing them to prepare writings, the matter of which was to be taken from the Bible, which they might consult for their improvement, instead of searching the Holy Scriptures for their edification. Equally unreasonable would it be to suppose, that the apostolic direction, with regard to singing psalms, could be understood by the primitive Christians, as authorizing them to prepare psalms to be used in the worship of God, instead of those which He himself had provided in His word. As the command of Christ, 'Search the Scriptures,' supposes that there were in existence sacred writings, with which those to whom the command was addressed, were acquainted, so the apostolic direction, 'sing psalms,' supposes that there were psalms in existence, which those to whom the direction was given, were to use. Those Christians to whom the words of the Apostle James were originally addressed, knew full well, that among the sacred writings which God had given to His church, there was a 'Book of Psalms.' And the exhortation to sing psalms would naturally be understood by them, as a direction to make use of the psalms which the Spirit of infinite wisdom had already provided. And in what sense would the Hebrew Christians understand the words of the Apostle, when he exhorted them to offer continually the sacrifice of praise to God? These Hebrews knew full well, how important it was that in all their offerings, those things only should be presented on the altar which God himself had appointed. They knew, moreover, that God himself had prepared and given to His church, a divine collection of psalms, and hymns, and songs, to be employed in singing His praise. And knowing these things, can it be supposed, that they would feel at liberty to lay aside those songs which God had prepared, and undertake to provide others more suitable for themselves? Can we for a moment entertain the thought, that they could understand the Apostle as authorizing them to disregard the lamb which God had provided as an offering for Himself, and to come before the Lord with the blind, the halt, and the lame? Had they presumed to do so, would they not have cause to apprehend the execution of the sentence, 'Cursed be the deceiver, which hath in his flock a male, and voweth and sacrificeth to the Lord a corrupt thing?' (Malachi i. 14.)

"And in addition to this consideration, it deserves to be particularly noticed, that while there is no Book of Psalms in the New Testament, there is no intimation whatever that one was needed; nor is there either a direction given to any man to furnish such a book, nor a single promise of the influences of the Holy Spirit to assist any man in preparing one. Under the former dispensation, God raised up a 'sweet Psalmist of Israel' whom he endowed with the gifts of the Holy Spirit, and eminently qualified for the important service. And by the instrumentality of a man, whom God called to the work and fitted for it, a collection of sacred songs has been communicated to the church, which Christians all over the world, in every age, have found from comfortable experience, to be admirably adapted to the end for which it was given. And when our glorious Lord, with whom is the residue of the Spirit, arose from the dead and ascended up far above all heavens that He might fill all things; and gave some evangelists, and some pastors and teachers; for the perfecting of the saints, for the edifying of the body of Christ; if it had been necessary for the edification of His church, it is not reasonable to suppose that among other gifts, He would have conferred the Spirit of Psalmody? But among the various services to which different individuals were called by the Head of the Church, and for which He qualified them, by imparting to them the gifts of the Holy Spirit, the preparation of a system of psalmody, for the edifying of the body of Christ, is never mentioned. Though with Him is the residue of the Spirit, it was not His pleasure to raise up and anoint a 'sweet Psalmist of Israel,' under the New Testament dispensation. And why was no one called to this important office? The only rational answer which can be given, is, that He in whom are hid all the treasures of wisdom and knowledge, did not consider it necessary. However liberal He may be in the distribution of His gifts, He bestows none that are unnecessary. And, having already made provision for the edification of His church, by furnishing her with a Book of Psalms, He did not call any of those, whom after His ascension, He endowed with the gifts of the Spirit, to provide another. Since, then, we are in the New Testament commanded to sing psalms, but never directed to *make psalms*, we come to the conclusion, that we have the sanction of the King of Zion, authorizing the use of the psalms, and hymns, and songs, which had already been furnished, for the edifying of the body of Christ.

"It may, however, be said, that these considerations, at most, prove nothing more than that we should employ the songs of Scripture in the worship of God; but will not establish the position, that the church should be confined to the use of those songs which are contained in the Book of Psalms. As to this I remark:

"That from the fact that God has given His church a Book of Psalms, it would appear to be the divine will that this should be used to the exclusion of all others. We have already had occasion to remark, that in ancient days, on various occasions, individuals, under the influence of the Spirit of inspiration, gave expression to the gratitude of their hearts, in a song of praise. Such songs of praise are found in various parts of the Bible. But, in process of time, a great variety of songs, composed by different men on various occasions, were collected together into one book, which not only has a place in the volume of inspiration, but to which God himself has given a peculiar title, 'The book of Psalms,' or songs of praise. The peculiar title of the book designates the end for which it was specially intended. And it is a fact which deserves particular notice, that some of the songs contained in the Book of Psalms, are found likewise in other parts of the Bible. The eighteenth psalm is found in the second book of Samuel, and the ninety-sixth, and the parts of some other psalms, are found in the second book of Chronicles. Other songs, such as the song of Moses at the Red sea, the song of Deborah and Barak and others, found in different parts of the Bible, are not transferred to the Book of Psalms. And the question naturally arises, Why is this distinction made? Why are some of those songs, which are found in other parts of the Bible, introduced likewise into the Book of Psalms, while others have no place in that collection? I can conceive of no answer so satisfactory as this; that the Book of Psalms being designed for permanent use in the worship of God, those songs have a place in this book, which, in the estimation of Infinite Wisdom, were best adapted to the edification of the church in all ages.

"It appears then, that in the Old Testament, the

duty of praising God by singing psalms or songs, is distinctly recognised : on various occasions, men who were moved by the Holy Ghost, furnished songs of praise appropriate to the circumstances of the church of God. Among those whom God was pleased to employ in this service, David, the royal prophet, stands pre-eminently distinguished as the sweet Psalmist of Israel. In process of time, a choice and varied collection of sacred songs, composed by different inspired men, on a variety of occasions, was given to the church by the God of Israel; to which collection of divine songs, He himself has appended the title, THE BOOK OF PSALMS. These songs are not the effusions of pious, well-meaning, but fallible men; they are the productions of the Holy Spirit, who spake by the mouth of his servants, the prophets. In these sacred hymns we have not an exhibition of human views of divine truth, which may be correct or may be erroneous; but we have the word of God itself, which is pure as silver tried in a furnace of earth, purified seven times. The praises of God are exhibited in these divine songs, not in the words which man's wisdom teacheth, but which the Holy Ghost teacheth. That God will accept the ascriptions of praise which are given to Him in these psalms, we are absolutely certain; because in them His Spirit has taught us to ascribe to Him the glory which is due unto His name.

"We pass on to the New Testament, and we find our Lord and His Apostles not only recognising the duty, but setting an example of praising God. What particular psalms and hymns they used, we are not expressly told; but every part of the New Testament furnishes evidence of their familiarity with the Book of Psalms. And that He in whom dwelt all the fulness of the Godhead bodily, and His Apostles who were endued with power from on high, did not use the effusions of uninspired men in the worship of God, is certain. In an interview with the Apostles, after His resurrection, our Lord addressed them in the following words:—' These are the words that I spake unto you, while I was yet with you, that all things must be fulfilled, which were written in the law of Moses, and in the prophets, *and in the psalms,* concerning Me.' From this and other declarations of like character in the New Testament, we have infallible evidence, that Jesus Christ himself is the great subject of the Book of Psalms. This the Apostles understood, when their divine Master opened their understandings, that they might understand the Scriptures; and the same thing will be understood by all who are taught of the Lord. And when we consider how frequently the Apostles introduce the psalms in their discourses and epistles, we cannot doubt that they regarded the matter of these sacred songs as very suitable to be employed in the worship of God. One thing, however, is certain, that neither our Lord nor His Apostles have furnished any psalms or songs in the New Testament, for the use of the church, much less have they provided a Book of Psalms. And further, there is no appointment given to any man to furnish psalms to be employed in the worship of God, nor is there a promise of the Spirit of Psalmody, to assist any one in performing this important service."*

III. These considerations and arguments acquire no little force from the fact, generally acknowledged, that *the church of Christ is one and the same* under both Testaments—the Old and the New. She is the "good olive tree" (Rom. xi.) from which the Jews were separated as decayed and barren branches, and into which the Gentiles have been "grafted." Some of the outward garniture of this one church was, it is true, removed at the advent, death, and resurrection of Jesus Christ. The *mode* of dispensing the Gospel was, in a measure, changed. Types, ceremonies, rites, —all of which had reference to the Messiah as their

---

* Pressly on Psalmody, pp. 83—90

antitype and substance—passed away, having answered the end of their institution; but the truth remains, the law remains. We still worship the same Jehovah, through the same Mediator, by the same spirit. The ten commandments are still the summary rule of human duty and obligation. The history of the Old Testament is now, as ever, the history of God's providential dealings with men, with nations, and with the church. The Book of Proverbs is yet the book of inspired maxims of wisdom, prudence, and purity. The prophecies are the peculiar inheritance of the New Testament dispensation. All those portions of the Word of God which " came of old time" are given to the church in all ages, for the *very same ends* of instruction, admonition, and consolation, which they were intended to subserve when first revealed and set in order by the instrumentality of men of God, who " spake as they were moved by the Holy Ghost." " For whatsoever things were written aforetime, were written for our learning, that we through patience and comfort of the Scriptures might have hope." (Rom. xv. 4.) And again, " All Scripture is given by inspiration of God, and is profitable for doctrine, for reproof, for correction, for instruction in righteousness: that the man of God may be perfect, thoroughly furnished unto all good works." (2 Tim. iii. 16, 17.)

If then other Scriptures are given for *our* use and profit, each part according to its own *proper nature and end*, why not the Book of Psalms, also, for all time, as a Book of Psalms, to be sung as appointed of God for *this very purpose*, just as truly as the Decalogue was given to be the summary of human duty to the end of the world? Once given to the church to be used in celebrating God's praise, where is the act setting it aside, any more than the Decalogue? Where the warrant to introduce other psalms or hymns to supersede this inspired and appointed manual? And, finally, these inquiries are the more pertinent and suggestive, in view of the fact that this book contains, as we have already proved, *all* that the church, requires for her exercises of sacred praise in song.

CHAPTER III.

IS THERE ANY WARRANT FOR MAKING OR USING IN THE WORSHIP OF GOD, PSALMS OR HYMNS, OTHER THAN THOSE ALREADY PROVIDED BY GOD FOR HIS CHURCH?

WE here consider—

I. The arguments employed in defence of the use of uninspired hymns. And,

I. *It is affirmed that these have a Scripture sanction.*

(1.) The "sayings" of Mary (Luke i. 46—55,) and the *prophecy* of Zecharias (Luke i. 68—79,) are regarded as "precedents" which imply such a sanction. This, they certainly are not. For of Mary, it is merely stated, that she "*said.*" Her utterances are not styled a *song;* nor is there any evidence that either she herself, or any other, then sang them. They are no more than a hearty outburst of thanksgiving—and no doubt inspired. As to Zecharias, it is said, he was " filled with the Holy Ghost and *prophesied.*" We are utterly unable to see how this can be construed into a warrant for the making of songs for the church by uninspired men, who do not even profess to " prophesy !" Moreover, all this was under the Old Testament economy, and not under the New.

(2.) Reference is made to the fact that our Saviour and His disciples " sang an hymn, and went out into the Mount of Olives." (Matt. xxvi. 30.) Were it admitted, or proved, that this " hymn" was made for the occasion by our Saviour, or by one of the Apostles, what authority would thus be furnished for the making of hymns by mere men, and these uninspired? Certainly, none at all. But this "hymn," it is now almost universally acknowledged, was the "Great Hallel," consisting of a number of consecutive psalms, which we now find in their order, in the Book of Psalms, and always sung at the close of the paschal feast. Dr. Clarke, himself an advocate for the use of uninspired hymns, says, "As to the *hymn* itself, we know from the universal consent of Jewish antiquity, that it was composed of Psalms 113, 114, 115, 116, 117 and 118, termed by the Jews HALLEL, from HALLELU-JAH, the first word in Psalm 113th. These six psalms were always sung at every paschal solemnity. They sung this great *hallel* on account of the five great benefits referred to in it; namely—1. The exodus from Egypt. 2. The miraculous division of the Red sea. 3. The promulgation of the law. 4. The resurrection of the dead. 5. The passion of the Messiah."*

(3.) A warrant for the use of uninspired compositions is sought in Eph. v. 19, and Col. iii. 16—and on these the advocates of "hymns" lay the greatest stress. That these passages will not bear the interpretation put upon them as enjoining, or favouring the use of uninspired songs, is thus satisfactorily shown by Dr. Cooper.

"It is admitted by those who urge these passages as authorizing the use of other songs than those contained in the Word of God, that the 'Psalms' which we are here enjoined to sing are the psalms of inspiration. We have the highest authority for regarding it as an admitted fact, that the psalms here referred to are the Psalms of David. We have the authority of the editors of the Princeton Repertory, a work published under the auspices, and sustained by the patron-

---

* For further allusions to this subject, see quotation from Dr. Cooper on Eph. v. 19, &c.

age, of the Old School Presbyterian Church, and edited by men of superior learning and talent. In the vol. for 1829, the editors say, in an article entitled 'The Sacred Poetry of the Early Christians': 'We can hardly conceive it possible that the Psalms of David could have been so generally adopted in the churches, and so highly esteemed by the best of the fathers, unless they had been introduced and sanctioned by the Apostles and inspired teachers.' Again, they say: 'It seems more correspondent to Scripture usage to consider the term psalms here as meaning the Book of Psalms, as used in Luke xxiv. 44, and equivalent to βιβλος ψαλμων Luke xx. 42, Acts i. 20, to which the New Testament writers so frequently refer for prophecies, proofs, and illustrations of their facts and doctrines.' In another part of the same article, the reader will find the following remark, which will, no doubt, commend itself to his good sense: 'As the first Christians were drawn from the synagogue, they naturally brought with them those songs of Zion which were associated with their earliest recollections and best feelings, and appropriated them to the services of the New Dispensation.' Olshausen, in his Commentary on Eph. v. 19, says: 'ψαλμοι (psalms) are probably here the psalms of the Old Testament, which passed from the synagogue into the church service.' Bengel also calls them the Psalms of David. In addition to this we may adduce the fact that the book of Dr. Watts is professedly made upon an admission that the psalms here mentioned by the Apostle are somehow or other the Psalms of David, for we have in this collection one hundred and fifty psalms which were doubtless made on this presumption. We then, surely, have the very best reasons for coming to the conclusion that all parties are agreed that the Apostle here refers to the Psalms of David. Indeed, the denial of this would be attended with so many difficulties that we do not apprehend, that the friends of human compositions will be disposed to take any other position. We wish the reader, in the subsequent discussion, to bear this in mind.

"The true and only question then before us is—Have we any reason for supposing that the 'hymns' and 'spiritual songs' here mentioned, are any thing different from the 'psalms'? It will not do to assume a difference. That difference must be proved in order to justify a resort to these passages as authorizing the use of anything else than the Book of Psalms. The reader will notice here, that the burden of proof rests on those who take the position, that the hymns and spiritual songs here mentioned, *are such as are not contained in the word of God.* Here is the very question at issue between us and our brethren. It is apprehended that multitudes interpret these passages under the force of their own practice, and the preconceived views upon which that practice is based. For instance, they are using, and have been from their earliest recollections, using a book containing religious devotional poems under the distinct head of 'psalms,' bearing, in point of number, an exact correspondence with the Divine collection, and also in point of sentiment some resemblance to it. In addition to these, there is also a large number that are published under the head of 'hymns.' As these are always called hymns, and the others psalms, the idea associated with the former word, as it occurs in these passages, is, that they are something like what is found in *their* book. Very little reflection, however, must suffice to show any person, that as these passages were written by the Apostle many centuries before the existence of any hymn-book now in use, so we must go to some other source if we would ascertain the idea attached to this word by the Apostle when directing us to sing not only psalms but hymns. The question for you, reader, to answer, is just this—How do you know, and what reason have you to give, that the *hymns mentioned by the Apostle* are not those which are contained in the word of God, instead of this hymn-book of yours which was made ten, twenty, or fifty years ago? Now, if you can present nothing more than the simple fact that in your book they are called hymns, you must at once see that you have nothing that in the least affects the question of Divine authority.

"Perhaps you will be ready to say, are the 'psalms, and hymns, and spiritual songs,' mentioned by the Apostle, only different names for the same things? Suppose we say, yes? How will you prove that they are not? How will you prove that any one of the inspired collection is not a hymn, or a spiritual song? If you deny it, be so good as to give a good reason for it. The only reason that I can conceive of as capable of being given by you is, that they are called by different *names*. Well, be so good as to tell us the difference between statutes, and judgments, and commandments, in the following passage, 1 Kings vi. 12 : 'If thou wilt walk in my statutes, and execute my judgments, and keep all my commandments, to walk in them ; then will I perform my word with thee.' Here are different names, and do they not relate to the same things? Are not God's statutes His judgments, and are they not both His commandments? But suppose we say no, they do not mean the same thing: psalms are not just the same as hymns, and hymns are not just the same as spiritual songs. What then? Why it appears that there is a difference. But the question still recurs, what is that difference? Is it the difference which exists between what is inspired, and what is not inspired? Do you not plainly see that unless you prove such a difference as this, you have not touched the question at issue between us? We may imagine a thousand differences, but they have no relevancy to the point before us, unless they go to show that these names are designed to express what is inspired and what is not inspired. Now, reader, this you never can do. You may try it as long as you please ; but you will fail in every effort. This you will see to be the case before we are through with the examination of this passage.

"Here we might with the greatest confidence leave the whole question; God has given to His church a book of praise, and a due regard for Him as its author, requires its use until those who offer us some other book, on the ground that He requires us to sing hymns and spiritual songs, show us that hymns and spiritual songs are not to be found in this book.

"But have the friends of an inspired psalmody nothing to support their position, that the Apostle, by these three terms, refers to the same thing, or at least that he does not, by hymns and spiritual songs, mean those which are not inspired? In order that the reader may judge of this, we shall submit to his candid attention the following considerations:—

(1.) "The difference contended for by the advocates of human psalmody is not practically observed by themselves. The Old School Presbyterian Church has taken metrical translations of the twenty-third and hundreth psalms, and placed them among their 'hymns.' Let the reader compare these psalms with the prose translation, and we are satisfied that he will at once acknowledge that if there can be such a thing as a metrical translation of the psalms, they may with the greatest propriety be so called. Surely if there be one among the one hundred and fifty of Dr. Watts' that may be called a psalm, these two deserve the name of 'psalms.' Let me ask, then, Are these two metrical translations of the Psalms of David, hymns? So have the General Assembly declared. Why may not the rest be called by the same name?

(2.) "If there be a distinction between the psalms and hymns, we are bound by the same mode of interpretation to suppose a distinction between the hymns and spiritual songs. But can the reader tell us what this distinction is? Let a hymn or spiritual song be read from their collection, and who can tell to which class it belongs. I may here refer to the practice of those who use hymns of human composition, to show that no such distinction is recognised. I have now before me the Hymn Book now in use in the Old School Presbyterian Church. In looking over it, I find a collection called 'Psalms,' consisting of one hundred and fifty. I find also a collection called 'Hymns,' consisting of six hundred and eighty. But where is the collection called 'Spiritual Songs?' They are not in the book. What plainer proof could we have that no such a distinction as the one contended for is recognised even by those churches that make use of human compositions in the worship of God? Will brethren expect us to recognise a distinction which they themselves practically ignore? Perhaps it may be said that the collection of 'Doxologies' in this book are intended as 'Spiritual Songs.' If so, they are not so designated. We have what is called 'The Christian Doxology' immediately after the 'Psalms.' To which of these do they belong? But this is not all, to show how utterly this distinction is ignored. The reader will find among these hymns some that are denominated *songs*. What could more conclusively show the utter groundlessness of the distinction which the advocates of human composition contend for, and which is made the basis of their interpretation of this passage?

(3.) "There are strong presumptions against recognising such a distinction as the one contended for. Either these hymns or spiritual songs were written by divine inspiration, or they were not. If they were thus written, then we have in this command a direction to sing an inspired psalmody, the very thing for which we contend. But what is the conclusion to which this admission brings us, on the supposition that these hymns and spiritual songs are not found in the Scriptures? The necessary conclusion is, that a part of the inspired writings has been lost, a conclusion to which we are sure the reader would be unwilling to come. The pious feelings of his heart would revolt against it. He will no doubt be ready to say with the editors of the Repertory, that 'It is not probable that any were written under the influence of inspiration, or they would have been preserved with other inspired writings.' Suppose, however, we take the other position, and say, with these editors, 'That men of education, genius and piety, employed their talents in the composition of hymns and spiritual odes, which, being approved by the Apostle, were introduced into the services of the church.' Then—leaving altogether out of view the important fact that we have not now the Apostles to whose judgment we can submit our uninspired hymns, and that they do not profess to have the *imprimatur* of these holy men—four difficulties present themselves to the mind: *(a.)* Why is it that we have not, in any of the Scriptures, the least allusion to the *making* of hymns and spiritual odes by these men 'of education, genius and piety?' On this subject there reigns throughout the Scriptures the stillness of the grave. Is not this strange, especially when we consider the importance of praise as a part of Divine worship, and the agitation which 'the introduction of hymns into the services of the church,' often produces at the present time? *(b.)* Is it reasonable to suppose that there would be found in the very infancy of the New Testament church a sufficient number of such men qualified to supply the church with these hymns and spiritual odes? Take these Ephesians, for instance. We know what they were before converted to Christianity. They were sunk in all the ignorance and pollution of idolatry, having been from their childhood worshippers of 'the great goddess Diana.' Without at all presuming to call in question the existence among them of men of education, genius and piety, we think it is by no means an unreasonable supposition, that it would not have been safe to commit to men just converted from their idolatrous worship, and consequently but partially enlightened and established in the truth, the making 'of hymns and spiritual songs,' in which to celebrate the praises of Jehovah. To our mind it would seem to be a dangerous experiment. (*c.*) The making of hymns by uninspired men, would, in all probability, produce difficulties between the Hebrew and Gentile Christians. In the language of the editors of the Repertory, 'The Hebrew Christians had probably been accustomed from childhood to consider inspired psalms alone admissible in the worship of the sanctuary, and cherished a holy and even superstitious dread of every thing like innovation or departure from the good old customs of their fathers.' Is it probable, that under these circumstances, the Apostle would direct to the use of uninspired hymns, when they had 'those songs of Zion which were associated with all their earliest recollections and best feelings?' And if the direction in regard to hymns and spiritual songs were only designed for the Gentile Christians, would not their introduction be calculated to keep up a bad state of feeling between these two classes of Christians, who were so disposed to cherish unfriendly feelings towards each other? (*d.*) The strongest presumption, however, that presents itself to our mind against this interpretation is, that it places uninspired compositions upon a par with those which are inspired. Here we have, according to this view, the Apostle associating, in the most intimate connexion, that which is confessedly the word of God, with the word of man; and not only so, but directing it to be used for the same end. Now, we would address ourselves to that reverence which the Christian reader cherishes for the word of God, and ask him whether an interpretation involving such a presumption as this, is reasonable? Were we to hear him giving an affirmative answer to this question, we must say we would receive it with no little surprise.

(4.) Another evidence in favour of supposing the

Apostle by these three terms to mean the same thing, is the fact that they are so employed by English, Greek, and Hebrew writers who are not inspired, and also by the inspired writers. A multitude of instances might be given, but we shall confine ourselves to a few. In the preface to a late work entitled 'The Psalms of David, translated by J. A. Alexander, Professor in the Theological Seminary at Princeton,' the reader will find the following remarks: 'A still more marked resemblance is, that they (the Psalms) are all not only poetical, but lyrical, *i.e.* songs, poems, intended to be sung, and with a musical accompaniment. Thirdly, they are all religious lyrics, even those which seem at first sight the most secular in theme and spirit, but which are all found on inquiry to be strongly expressive of religious feeling. In the fourth place, they are all ecclesiastical lyrics, psalms or hymns, intended to be permanently used in the worship of God, not excepting those which bear the clearest impress of original connexion with the social, domestic, or personal relations and experience of the writers.' Now, we have this learned and highly esteemed Professor declaring not only that the Psalms of David are *all intended to be permanently used in the public worship of God* (a remark worthy the attention of the reader), but also that they are all songs and hymns. Will this language be justified? Then why suppose that the Apostle means anything else by these terms, but the same Psalms of David; and why represent those who confine the matter of their praise to these psalms as opposing the use of hymns and spiritual songs? Josephus refers to the Psalms of David under the name of songs and hymns. The Apostolic Canons contain this injunction: ' Ετερος τους του Δαβιδ ψαλλετω υμνους και ο λαος τα ακροστιχια υποψαλλετω. Let another sing the hymns of David, and let the people repeat the concluding lines.' Here we have not only a proof of the very great antiquity of the use of David's Psalms in the Christian Church, but also a proof that they were known by the name of hymns—the very same name in the original which the Apostle employs in the text. Dr. Gill tells us that they are spoken of in the Talmud by the name of 'songs and praises, or hymns.' Let us now open the sacred Scriptures, and here we shall find proof to the same effect. We find the psalms called 'Sepher Tehillim' (the Hymn Book), in the very title of the Hebrew copy of the Psalms. The 145th Psalm is called Tehilla l' David, which Gesenius translates 'a hymn of David.' The same term is frequently introduced into the body of the psalm. Let the reader compare Psalm 22d and verse 23d of the Hebrew, with the Greek of Hebrews ii. 12, and he will find the declaration of the Psalmist, 'In the midst of the congregation I will praise thee' [ahalleka], rendered by the apostle, [$'ὑμνήσω$] 'I will sing a hymn to thee.' The word Halleluja, which so frequently occurs in the Psalms, is just a call to sing a hymn to the Lord. Other illustrations of this might be given, but let these suffice. Now, when we find the sacred writers, and among these the Apostle himself, using this very term 'hymn' in application to the songs of inspiration, is it not fair to infer that he used it with the same application in the passage before us? But this is not all. It is generally supposed that the Apostle made use of the Septuagint version of the Scriptures. With this version the Ephesians and Colossians, being Greeks, were no doubt familiar. Let us open then this version of the Psalms, and we will find some of them bearing the title of a psalm, others of a hymn, and others of a song exactly corresponding to the three Hebrew titles, Mizmar, Tehilla, and Shir. These words in the Septuagint are the very same as those which are employed by the Apostle when he directs the Ephesians and Colossians to 'sing psalms, hymns, and spiritual songs.' Will the reader then look at this, and ask himself whether the probabilities in favour of our interpretation of this passage, are not such as almost to amount to a moral certainty. We may just remark, that the editors of the Repertory say, vol. 7, page 76, 'External evidence places the titles of the Psalms precisely on the same foundation with the Psalms themselves.' Professor Alexander, of Princeton, says, 'They are found in the Hebrew text as far as we can trace its history, not as *addenda*, but as intregral parts of the composition.'

(5.) "Another consideration which makes it highly probable that the Book of Psalms is intended by the Apostle, is the fact that the same language is employed by the evangelist in Matthew xxvi. 30, where he tells us that the Saviour and His disciples at the celebration of the passover sang a hymn ; ['υμνησαντες, *they having hymned.*'] That a portion of the Psalms of David was used, is almost universally admitted. Indeed there is hardly any thing upon which commentators seem to be more generally agreed than this. The evidence in its behalf is as strong as it well could be without being positively asserted by the historian. The writings of the Jews abound with testimony to prove that it was their custom during that solemnity to sing the six Psalms of David, beginning with the 113th, and ending with the 118th. There is no evidence that a hymn was made for the occasion, and we know that it was His custom to comply with the observances of the Jews, of which this was one part, and certainly a most appropriate part. Now if it be admitted that the hymn sung by our Saviour and His disciples on this most affecting occasion was an inspired hymn, we argue, from this admission, that the hymns referred to by the Apostle in these passages belonged to the same inspired collection. If this inspired collection was used by our Lord and His disciples, the presumption is, in absence of all proof to the contrary, that they would still continue to be used by the disciples. That this admission is made by those who use uninspired compositions, we have only to refer to Mr. Barnes. He says on this passage, 'The passover was observed by the Jews by singing, or chanting, the 113th, 114th, 115th, 116th, 117th and 118th Psalms. There can be no doubt that our Saviour and the Apostles also, used the same Psalms in their observance of the passover.' Why then doubt that the Apostle referred to the same collection when he told the Ephesians to 'sing hymns?' Surely if any argument can be drawn from the *usus loquendi* of the sacred writers, it is on the side of those who maintain that the reference in this passage is to the Psalms of divine inspiration.

(6.) In the preceding remarks we have looked simply at the names employed by the Apostle in designating that which he would have these Ephesians and Colossians to sing. We now request the reader to give us his attention while we present to his consideration some additional evidence, drawn from the language employed by the Apostle in connexion with the use of of these three terms. (*a.*) These songs are called '*spiritual* songs,' ['ωδαι πνευματικαι.] The heathen made use of odes. In order to distinguish those which the Apostle would have them to use, he calls them 'spiritual.' Now we apprehend that there is, in the use of this term, a proof that the songs referred to by the Apostle were those contained in the Scriptures. If the reader will take the pains, as we have done, to examine those places in the New Testament Scriptures where this word occurs, he will find that in every instance where the reference is not to created spirits, there is a distinct reference to the Spirit of God as the atuhor of that to which the term is applied. Thus 'spiritual gifts' are such as are communicated directly by the Spirit. We shall here quote the words of Mr. Barnes on the word 'spiritual,' as it occurs in 1 Cor. x. 3, 4, ' And did all eat of the same spiritual meat, and did all drink of the same spiritual drink, for they drank of that spiritual rock that followed them.' 'The word spiritual here,' says Mr. Barnes, 'is evidently used to denote that which was given by the Spirit, or by God; that which the result of His miraculous gift, and which was not produced by the ordinary way, and which was not the gross food on which men are usually supported. It had an excellency and value from the fact that it was the immediate gift of God, and thus called angels' food. Ps. lxxviii. 25. It is called by Josephus 'divine and extraordinary food.' [Antiq. 3. 1.] In the language of the Scriptures, that which is distinguished for excellence, which is the immediate gift of God, which is unlike that which is gross, and of earthly origin, is called *spiritual*, to denote its purity, value, and excellence; compare Rom. vii. 14; 1 Cor. iii. 1; xv. 44—46; Eph. i. 3. The idea of Paul here is, 'that all the Israelites were nourished and supported in this remarkable manner by food given directly by God.' Again he says, 'The word spiritual must be used in the sense of supernatural, or that which is immediately given by God.' In addition to the passages to which Mr. Barnes refers, let the reader consult Rom. i. 11; xv. 27; 1 Cor. ii. 13, 14, 15; ix. 11; xii. 1; xiv. 1—37; Gal. vi. 1; Col. i. 9. Now let this meaning be attached to the word in the passage before us, and we are brought to the conclusion that the songs here referred to by the Apostle, are those which were 'given by the Spirit, or by God,' which were 'not produced in the ordinary way,' but which were 'bestowed in a miraculous and supernatural manner,' and where will we find such songs but those which are contained in the Scriptures? In singing the Psalms of David, we know that we are singing such songs, for He himself tells us, that 'the Spirit of the Lord spake by him, and and His word was on his tongue.' That this is the import of the word *spiritual*, as here used, is rendered highly probable from the circumstance that the Apostle has expressly mentioned the Holy Spirit in the same sentence. (*b*.) Another reason for this interpretation is, that the Apostle directs to the use of these 'psalms, hymns, and spiritual songs' as the means of being 'filled with the Spirit.' Now, is not the word of God, the very word of God, the means which He makes use of in filling the hearts of His people? When the Saviour prayed that the Father would sanctify His disciples through His truth, He adds, 'Thy word is truth.' There we must go, if we would be filled with the Spirit. Out of these living wells we must draw water, with which to refresh our souls. (c.) We find that the Apostle directs to the singing of psalms, hymns, and spiritual songs, as the means of letting 'the word of Christ dwell in them richly, in all wisdom.' Guyse has a sermon on this text, entitled, 'The Scriptures the word of Christ.' This he shows from three considerations. 'He is its author;' 'He is its great subject;' and 'He works and carries on His interest by it.' 'The Spirit of Christ,' we are told, 'was in the prophets, when they testified beforehand of the sufferings of Christ and the glory that should follow,' and it is said, ' He went and preached to the spirits in prison;' so that the Psalms of David may, with the greatest propriety, be called 'the word of Christ.' 'There is not,' says Bishop Horsely, ' a page of this Book of Psalms, in which the pious reader will not find his Saviour, if he reads with a view of finding Him.' 'We are in these Psalms,' (says Dr. Russell, in his admirable letters,) ' brought, as it were, into his closet, are made the witnesses of his secret devotions, and are enabled to see even the inward workings of his heart.' Guyse, in the sermon before referred to, infers that the ' word of Christ,' as here mentioned by the Apostle, includes not only the New, but also the Old Testament Scriptures. He remarks, ' It is in this most extensive view, that our Apostle seems to take it, by his speaking, in the remainder of the verse of teaching and admonishing one another in psalms, and hymns, and spiritual songs, which look with a very strong aspect toward the Old Testament writings, some of which are set forth under these titles.' Add to this the consideration that but a part of the New Testament Scriptures was written at this time, so that we may readily suppose that the reference of the Apostle is to the 'psalms, hymns, and spiritual songs' of the Old Testament Scriptures. At all events they must be such as belonged to the Scriptures, and this is all for which we are now contending. Now, the reader will observe, that it is this 'word' (not simply the principles of this word, but the word itself), which the Apostle would have these Ephesians to let dwell in them, by singing psalms, and hymns, and spiritual songs. Is not this more likely to be done by singing the sacred songs of this word, than by singing those which have been composed by erring man, whatever may be his piety and learning? Is it not more likely that we shall in this way attain to that 'wisdom' of which the Apostle speaks in the same passage? We know how it was with David; 'I have more understanding,' he could say, 'than all my teachers, for *thy testimonies* are my meditation.'

" We have thus given these two passages a careful and critical examination. In this examination nothing has been assumed—not a single idea in the whole process of exposition has been advanced without a reason having been assigned for it. The points have been distinctly presented so that the reader can examine each of these points for himself, as it is laid before him. We now submit this exposition to the candid consideration of all who may desire to know the mind of God as revealed in His word, and with whom, in judging of matters pertaining to the worship of God, the great question ever is, *What saith the Scripture?*

" Having subjected these passages to what we believe to be a faithful and impartial examination, it may not be out of place to inquire how far the result harmonizes with the views of distinguished divines and commentators. A careful inquiry will show that those who maintain that the hymns and spiritual songs mentioned by the Apostle are those of inspiration, have clearly the weight of authority on their side.

"In an edition of the Westminster version of the Psalms, published in 1673, the reader will find a preface signed by the celebrated Dr. Owen, and twenty-five others, among whom are to be found the most illustrious divines that have ever adorned the church. Their testimony on the point before us is given in the following words: 'To us David's Psalms seem plainly intended by these terms of psalms, and hymns, and spiritual songs, which the Apostle useth. Eph. v. 19; Col. iii. 16.'

"Ridgely, in his Body of Divinity, expresses the same view, and says: 'It cannot be denied that the Psalms of David are called indifferently by these names.'

"Dr. Gill, the learned Calvinistic divine of the Baptist school, in the introductory remarks to his Commentary on the Book of Psalms, says: 'To these several names of this book, the Apostle manifestly refers in Eph. v. 19, Col. iii. 16.' In his exposition of Eph. v. 19, he thus expresses himself: 'The hymns are only another name for the Book of Psalms,' and ' by spiritual songs are meant the same Psalms of David, Asaph, &c.'

"Calvin, according to Doddridge, in his note to Col. iii. 16, 'thinks all these words refer to David's poetical pieces.'

"Beza, according to Macknight, 'thinks *psalms* in this passage denote those poetical compositions in which David uttered his complaints and prayers; also those historical narratives by which he instructed the people; and *hymns* are his other compositions in which he celebrated the praises of God.'

"Macknight limits the 'psalms, and hymns, and spiritual songs, mentioned by the Apostle, to those which were 'recorded in the Scripture,' and to such as were 'dictated by the Spirit.' The same view is expressed by the continuators of Henry's Commentary, and by Bloomfield, Brown, Horne, Durham, Daillé, and others.

"The reader will see from the authorities to which we have referred, that our criticisms on these passages *present them in no new light to the church.* Indeed, we question whether any one of the evangelical denominations can find anything like the same authority, either in point of weight or variety, for their interpretation of any of the proof texts on which they rest anything that is *distinctive* in their profession, either in relation to doctrine, worship, or government."

I. Some use is made in defending "hymns" of Isaiah xxvi. 1: "In that day shall this song be sung in the land of Judah," &c. It is obvious, however, to remark, (1.) That this, if a "song" literally intended to be sung, is an *inspired* one; how, then, can the language of the prophet be an argument for the use of *uninspired* hymns? At most, it can only touch the question, whether any Bible songs may be used in worship other than those contained in the Book of Psalms? (2.) If sung, it must be sung as given, in a literal translation, though metrical. Hence this passage contains no argument for even a paraphrase—using the term in its modern acceptation. But (3.) It is by no means certain that it was intended that this passage should be used as a part of the church's manual of praise: for had this been the design of the Spirit, how did it happen that this "song" was not introduced into the worship of the church from the earliest period, and continued down to our day? Surely there has been some strange oversight here! Whatever use has been made of this passage in song has been, so far as any testimony appears, of very late date. (4.) The prophecy has been accomplished, however, and the saints have used with gratitude this language in magnifying the power, and faithfulness, and mercy of Judah's Saviour and King, although they have not sung this passage in their exercises of devotion. (5.) Have the advocates of "hymns" given this song any prominent place in their public praises?

We cannot find the Scripture warrant which is claimed for uninspired songs in God's worship. The Bible gives them no sanction.

II. It is affirmed that such hymns and songs have

the sanction of long and general use in the Christian church: and some have gone so far as to put hymn-singing under the rule, that what the people of God always, and in all places, have held is right; regarding the exceptions as so few, that they may be left entirely out of the account. In reply, we might content ourselves with the re-assertion of the principle which holds a high place in the estimation of the purest Protestants, namely, that the practice of the church is of small moment in settling any controversy in regard to faith or duty, unless we go as far back as apostolic times, and ascertain the apostolic sanction; or, in other words, except as we find these matters of faith and duty recorded or exemplified in the sacred Scriptures. We are persuaded, however, that those with whom we now reason can find no *such* use of hymns in the Christian church as implies the Divine approbation, or even until a late period, a full ecclesiastical sanction.

For greater distinctness in considering the subject, we divide the history of the church into three periods —the Primitive, the Mediæval, and the Reformed.

1. The Primitive, extending from the close of the first century, down to the fourth or fifth.* And here we state: (1.) That no hymn can be traced back to apostolic times. A late writer †—almost an enthusiast in reference to hymns, but who has carefully examined his ground, says, "Three Hymns have come down to us from early times." These are the "Tersanctus," the "Te-Deum," and the "Gloria in Excelsis." Of these, the "Te Deum" belongs to the later periods of the fourth century: of the "Tersanctus," or "Thrice

---

* Strictly taken, the limits of the Primitive Church, would be narrower than this.

† The author of a work entitled, "The Voice of the Christian Life in Song: or, Hymns and Hymn-writers of Many Lands and Ages," understood to be by a clergyman of the English Establishment. The edition from which we quote, is that of Robert Carter & Brother, New York, 1859.

Holy,' it is said that "all that can be discovered" is, that it "can be found in the earliest known liturgies:" and of the "Gloria in Excelsis" that it is "possibly or probably more ancient than any thing Clement of Alexandria, the earliest hymn-writer, ever wrote."* And of all the "Anonymous Greek Hymns," this writer says, "Whether, therefore, the greater purity of many of these anonymous hymns arises from their greater antiquity, or from a fresh approach to that ever-present Fountain in an age when many had recourse to polluted waters and broken cisterns, is a problem we may contentedly leave unsolved." Now had hymns been used with apostolic sanction, could they have so completely perished? No kind of literature is so certainly transmitted to future generations as songs. Is it possible, that songs which had been sung by the Apostles, and apostolic churches, should have so completely disappeared from the life and memory of the church? (2.) The Scripture Psalms were used from the earliest periods of the church, and the weight of evidence is in favour of their exclusive use in the apostolic church. The Biblical Repertory (1829), says, "From the Jewish synagogue, sacred music very naturally passed into the Christian sanctuary. Our Blessed Lord himself, on that memorable night when he instituted the sacramental memorial of his dying love, furnished the transition act by concluding the solemnity with a hymn.† As the first Christians were drawn from the synagogue, they naturally brought with them those Song of Zion, which were associated with all their earliest recollections and best feelings, and appropriated them to the service of the new dispensation." It adds, speaking of alleged changes of an early date, "In the hands of Apostles or Christian poets of apostolic times, we have no informa-

---

* Clement lived at the end of the second century.

† The Hillel, some portion of Psalms 113 to 118. Princeton Bib. Repertory for 1829.

tion. At a later period we find psalms in general use in the churches, and judged by the fathers the most estimable portion of their religious services. The Apostolical Canons contain the injunction: 'Let another sing the *hymns* of David, and let the people repeat the concluding lines.' We can hardly conceive it possible that the Psalms of David could have been so generally adopted in the churches, and so highly esteemed by the best of the fathers, unless they had been introduced or sanctioned by the Apostles and inspired teachers."* Neander, who without furnishing any direct proof of his statement, speaks of hymns at this early date, furnishes evidence in the following quotation against his own view, well suited to our purpose, " Besides the Psalms which had been used from the earliest times, and the short *doxologies* and *hymns* consisting of verses from the Holy Scriptures, spiritual songs, composed by distinguished church teachers, were also introduced among the pieces used for public worship, in the Western church. To the last named practice *much opposition*, it is true, was expressed. It was demanded, that, in conformity with the *ancient usage*, nothing should be used in the music of public worship, but what was taken from the *Sacred Scriptures*. As sectaries and heretical parties often had recourse to Church Psalmody to spread their own religious opinions, all those songs which had not been for *a long time* in use in the church, were particularly liable to suspicion."† In this, Neander is treating of a comparatively late period, and yet, even then the introduction of hymns, although written by " eminent teachers," was " opposed," and the " ancient practice" was acknowledged, and, it would seem, maintained to be, that nothing should be sung but what was " contained in the Sacred Scriptures." Hence, even these songs, which are said to have been " long in use,"

* Princeton Biblical Repertory for 1829.

† Hist. ii. 318.

unless they were Scripture Psalms, must have been introduced after the times then called "ancient," going back to the apostolic. The significant fact, however, is, that the introduction of "hymns" was, at that time, an innovation. (3.) The first known hymn-writer was Bardesanes, " a native of Ædessa, a man of mind, of a Gnostic sect, and of course a zealous opponent of the doctrine of the Godhead of Christ, in the second century.' He was among the first, if not the first, that was distinguished for the composition of new hymns. The Gnostic doctrines were poetic, and they were made popular, and widely extended by the *hymns* and *odes* of this heretical poet, and those of his more distinguished son, Harmonius, who, with his father, espoused the same bad cause. Bardesanes 'IMITATED David, that he might be adored and recommended by similar honours. For this purpose he composed 150 psalms.'* Into those psalms and hymns he infused his corrupt and mystic doctrines, rendering them agreeable to the taste of his readers ' by the charms of novelty, and the embellishments of oriental style.' And it is added, 'Thus the Syrian church was in danger of being overflowed with Gnostic errors through the mighty vehicle of song."† The next in order, is Clement, already mentioned. He wrote but *one* hymn, but whether to be sung, or whether it was sung in the worship of God at the time, is a thing unknown : we have seen no evidence that it was. (4.) We have, besides the clear testimony of Neander, ample evidence, some of which we have furnished in our first chapter, that the Psalms of Scripture were most highly regarded, and constantly used in the early church, while hymns were still regarded with suspicion. Augustine says—he is of the fourth century, " The Donatists, too, 'reproached the orthodox,'

---

* Ephræm the Syrian, as quoted by the Princeton Repertory of 1829, in an interesting article on "The Sacred Poetry of the Early Christians," p. 530.

† M'Master's Apology, pp. 44, 45.

' because they sung with sobriety the divine songs of the prophets, while they (the Donatists) inflamed their minds with the poetic effusions of human genius." In the Apostolic Constitutions* we learn that " the woman, the children, and the humblest mechanics, could repeat all the Psalms of David ; they chanted them at home and abroad ; they made them the exercises of their piety and the refreshment of their mind. Thus they had answers ready to oppose temptation, and were always prepared to pray to God, and to praise him, in any circumstance, *in a form of his own inditing.*' Cassian of the fifth century, says, " The elders have not changed the ancient custom of singing *psalms.* The devotions are performed in the same order as formerly. The *hymns* which it had been the custom to sing at the close of the night vigils, namely, the 50th, 62d, 89th, 148th, *Psalms,* &c., are the same *hymns* which are sung at this day." And as late as A.D. 561—563, the council of Braga forbid " the introduction of other poetry into the Psalmody of the church, beyond the songs of *canonical scripture.*"†

The history of this early period furnishes nothing of which the advocates of " hymns" attempt to make much use, excepting a passage in Pliny's letter to Trajan, early in the second century, and an extract from an epistle of the council of Antioch, A.D., 264, regarding a certain proceeding of Paulus of Samosata. Pliny says, that he had learned that the Christians of Bithynia " were wont to meet together on a stated day, before it was light, and sing among themselves alternately a

---

* Of these Dr. M'Master says, " The collection of regulations. known under the name of the ' Apostolical Constitutions,' made its appearance in the fourth century. Though we may justly dispute its apostolical origin, it may be admitted of sufficient authority. as far as it indicates the customs of the third and following century. We see its testimony respecting the use of the Book of Psalms."

† Ut extra psalmos vel scripturas canonicas nihil poetice compositum in ecclesia psallatur. M'Master, p. 65.

hymn to Christ as God," &c. But what, we ask with some astonishment, is there in this—even admitting that Pliny's *words* are the precise ones that a Christian would have used in speaking of their psalmody—to countenance the supposition that they sang uninspired compositions? Surely, the Psalms of the Bible exhibit Christ as a divine Person! Does not the apostle Paul take arguments from the Psalms (see Heb. i.) to demonstrate the proper divinity of the Son? Have not a host of Christians, past and present, found Christ in these Psalms, and worshipped Him, in singing them, as a divine Saviour? Nor was the early church ignorant on this subject, as will appear presently.

But, are not the *words* of a pagan pro-consul rather a slender foundation on which to build so large an edifice of hymn-singing? If hymns were then composed and sung—if this was the custom—if it had been consecrated, and the songs themselves in a sense, by the death of martyrs, we again ask, what has become of them, and why has it been left to subsequent ages to learn the fact that they existed from one rather vague sentence in a Roman pro-consul's letter? Certainly, we might look for some more direct and explicit knowledge of so important a fact, through some ecclesiastical channel! How much we have, has been seen already: or, more correctly, that we have nothing of the kind, through the testimony of the church herself.

As to Paul of Samosata, we allow Dr. Pressly to speak. "There is a passage of history in connexion with the life of Paul of Samosata, which has sometimes been referred to, for the purpose of establishing the conclusion that hymns of human composition were in general use in the primitive age, in the orthodox church, and that it was through the influence of heretical teachers, that the Psalms of David were introduced. It will at once occur to the reflecting Christian, that it would be something very strange, if it were really so, that the enemies of the truth should manifest a partiality for a portion of the word of God, which has always been peculiarly dear to the humble, practical Christian. But what are the facts in the case just referred to? Paul of Samosata, who rejected the doctrine of our Lord's divinity, has been represented as banishing from the church in Antioch 'the old church hymns, that spake of Christ as the incarnate Word,' and as introducing in their stead the Psalms of David, as being better adapted to the promotion of his heresy.

"That this portion of history, in so far as it stands connected with the subject of psalmody, may be set in its true light, I shall present to the reader an extract from the Epistle of the council of Antioch which condemned the heresy of Paul, together with the Latin translation of the learned Valesius. Our information with regard to this matter is derived from the proceedings of the Council. The original may be seen in Harduin's Acta Conciliorum, Tom. I., or in the History of Eusebius, Lib. 8 cap. 30.

ORIGINAL OF THE EPISTLE.

ψαλμους δε τους μεν εις τον Κυριον ημων Ιησουν Χριστον παυσας, ως δη νεωτερους, και νεωτερων ανδρων συγγραμματα. εις εαυτον δε, εν μεση τη εκκλησια τη μεγαλη τη πασχα ημερα, ψαλμωδειν γυναικας, Παρασκευαζων. ων και ακουσας τις φριξειεν.

TRANSLATION OF VALESIUS

"Quinetiam psalmos in honorum Domini Jesu Christi cani solitos, quasi novellos, et a recentioribus hominibus compositos, abolevit. Mulieres, autem magno paschæ die in media ecclesia, psalmos quosdam canere ad sui ipsius laudem instituit; quod quidem audientibus horrorem merito incusserit."

The scholar who examines the original, will see that the following is a literal translation. Paul "put a stop to the psalms in honour of our Lord Jesus Christ, as though (they had been) modern, and the compositions of modern men, and prepared women on the great

G

day of Easter, in the midst of the church, to sing psalms in honour of himself." It will be seen that this translation differs from that which has commonly been given, simply in the rendering of the particle ὡς. According to the more common interpretation of the passage, this particle has been understood in the sense of *because*. And hence, Paul is charged with setting aside the psalms which were sung in the church of Antioch, *because* they were modern.

"But, to say the least, it is not necessary that we should understand the particle in this sense. According to very common usage, it is employed to convey the idea of comparison or similitude, rather than to signify the reason for which a thing is done. Examples almost innumerable of the following kind occur in the New Testament—'Be ye wise *as* serpents, and harmless *as* doves.' Matt. x. 16. 'His raiment was white *as* the light.' 'If ye have faith *as* a grain of mustard seed.' Matt. xvii. 2, 20. 'He was led *as* a sheep to the slaughter; and *like* a lamb dumb before his shearer.' Acts viii. 32. And in Acts xxvii. 30, it is translated correctly, '*as though*,' as I believe it should be in the passage under consideration. In all such instances, it will be seen that this particle is used to convey the idea of comparison between objects which in some respects resemble each other.

"Understanding the particle in this sense, as employed by the council, the charge preferred against Paul is, that he took as much liberty with the psalms, which the church in Antioch had been accustomed to sing, *as though* they had been the compositions of modern men. And the implied idea is, that the psalms which had been sung in that church were not modern, nor the compositions of modern men, but were the songs of inspiration. And the daring impiety of Paul appeared in this, that he treated the divine songs which celebrate the praises of the Lord Jesus as though they had been the compositions of uninspired men.

"The council, then, according to this view, do not say that Paul set aside the psalms which had been sung at Antioch *because* they were the compositions of modern men, but, as *though* they had been of this character. This view, it will be seen, accords with the translation of Valesius. He employs the term ' *quasi*,' as though, to express the sense of the original.

"In support of this interpretation of the epistle of the council which condemned the heresy of Paul, the following considerations are submitted to the judgment of the unprejudiced reader:—

1. "The sacred songs, which the church in Antioch had been accustomed to sing, and the use of which Paul of Samosata is said to have abolished, are termed '*psalms*.' Neander, it is true, denominates them 'the church hymns which had been in use since the second century;' and others describe them as 'the old church hymns that spake of Christ as the incarnate Word.' But the council speaks of them as the '*psalms*.' Now, while I freely admit that this term does not conclusively establish the fact, that these sacred songs were the Psalms of David, yet it furnishes a strong presumptive argument in favour of this supposition. It will, I suppose, be admitted by all who are concerned in this controversy, that this term is more commonly used to designate the psalms of inspiration, and that it is not the term usually employed in reference to the compositions of uninspired men.

"But, perhaps, it will be said that, the qualifying phrase, psalms '*in honour of our Lord Jesus Christ*,' determines that they were songs composed by men for the purpose of testifying to the truth of our Lord's divinity. To this I reply, that such a conclusion is by no means legitimate. All that appears from the language of the council is, that the psalms which were sung in Antioch had reference to Christ, and were in honour of him. Now, if the Psalms of David do bear testimony to the divine dignity and glory of the Lord

Jesus Christ; and if they do speak of him as being a divine person, and yet as appearing in our world in human nature; and if the church, in the days of Paul of Samosata, thus understood the psalms, then it was strictly proper and natural for these advocates of the truth of our Lord's divinity to speak of the inspired psalms as being sung in honour of our Lord Jesus Christ.

"That the psalms do celebrate the glory of our Lord Jesus Christ; that they do exhibit him to the view of our faith, as a divine person, and at the same time, as a man of sorrows and acquainted with grief, it cannot be necessary that I should undertake to prove. It may be sufficient to refer to the numerous instances in which the psalms are applied to the Lord Jesus by the writers of the New Testament, and particularly to the declaration of our Lord himself, in which He says to His disciples, Luke xxiv. 44: 'These are the words which I spake unto you, while I was yet with you, that all things must be fulfilled which were written in the law of Moses and in the prophets, and in *the psalms*, concerning me.'

"And while it is perfectly evident that Jesus Christ, in His person and work; in His divine dignity, humiliation, sufferings and death; resurrection and ascension into heaven, is the great subject of the psalms, it is not less evident from the writings of the primitive Christians, that the psalms were thus understood by them. And this being the fact, it was perfectly natural for them, when speaking of these divine hymns, to represent them as being sung in honour of the Lord Jesus Christ. In confirmation of what has just been said with regard to the sense in which the psalms were understood by the primitive Christians, it may be sufficient for my purpose to adduce the testimony of Justin Martyr, who wrote about the middle of the second century. In his Dialogue with Trypho the Jew, in which the particular design of this learned father is to prove that Jesus Christ is the Messiah promised to the fathers, the psalms generally are referred to, as furnishing the proof of his position. For example, Justin quotes the 110th Psalm as applicable to the Messiah. And then addressing Trypho, he says: 'I am not ignorant that you Jews explain this psalm as though it referred to Hezekiah.' But he adds: 'The words themselves declare that it relates to our Jesus.' After having pointed out clearly the application of this psalm to the Lord Jesus Christ, Justin addressed Trypho in the following language: 'That I may convince you that ye Jews do not understand your own Scriptures, I will mention another psalm dictated to David by the Holy Spirit, which you contend was spoken with reference to Solomon, your king, but which, in reality, was uttered concerning our Christ.' It is the 72d Psalm to which Justin here refers; and after repeating the entire psalm he remarks: 'In the conclusion of this psalm it is written, *the hymns of David are ended.*' And then he proceeds to show that the things spoken in this psalm cannot apply to Solomon, as the Jews were wont to contend, but do relate to our Lord Jesus Christ.

"If, then, the primitive Christians understood the psalms as referring to the Lord Jesus, as is abundantly evident from the writings of Justin Martyr and others, it was strictly appropriate and natural, when speaking of them, to represent them as being sung in honour of Him. And the language applied to the psalms which were sung in Antioch in the days of Paul of Samosata, very correctly describes the Psalms of David, as they were understood in the primitive ages of Christianity.

"If it were necessary to adduce further proof in confirmation of what has been said in relation to the sense in which the psalms were understood by the primitive Christians, it would be easy to multiply testimonies from the writings of Irenæus, of Clement of Alexandria, of Athanasius, of Augustine, and others of similar character, who were distinguished advocates of the truth.

Indeed, these Fathers, instead of experiencing any difficulty in seeing their divine Redeemer in the psalms, appear, from their writings, to have had Him presented to the view of their faith everywhere throughout these sacred hymns.

2. "But that the Psalms, the use of which Paul abolished, were not 'the compositions of modern men,' and could not have been set aside by him under the pretext that they were 'modern,' will appear from this consideration: That which he is said to have introduced, would be equally, if not in a greater degree obnoxious, to the same objection. The psalms which he removed were such as were 'in honour of the Lord Jesus Christ;' those which he appointed to be sung in their stead were 'in honour of himself.' Now, it is certain that none of the Psalms of David would be adapted to the purpose of celebrating the praises of Paul of Samosata. And it is no less certain that any songs which were in honour of this enemy of the truth must have been modern, and the compositions of an uninspired man. And though Paul was a heretic, it cannot be supposed that he was so perfectly devoid of common sense as to urge as a reason for setting aside the existing psalmody of the church, a consideration which would apply with greater force to the exclusion of what he proposed to introduce.

"I am aware, that it has been customary to *suppose*, that Paul introduced the Psalms of David in the room of those which he displaced. Neander says, 'he *probably* suffered nothing but psalms to be used.' Others not quite so modest, assert without any qualification, that it was the 'pompous Unitarian, Paul of Samosata, who first set the example of installing the psalms in the place of exclusive dignity.' But where, I ask, is the authority for such conjectures, or for such unqualified affirmations? The Epistle of the Council, by whose authority the heresy of Paul was condemned, says no such thing.

"So far from it, the express declaration of the Council

is irreconcilable with such a supposition. The psalmody which, according to the Council, Paul introduced, was designed to celebrate his own praise ; was in honour of himself. And this could not have been an inspired psalmody, but must have been a system of which man was the author.

"The conclusion, then, to which I am conducted, taking the language of the Council as my guide, and not suffering myself to be misled by the mere conjectures and suppositions of men, may be exhibited in the following propositions :

1. "The psalmody employed in the worship of God in the church of Antioch, in the days of Paul of Samosata, was a divine system. The psalms which were sung at that time, were in honour of our Lord Jesus Christ And this character belongs appropriately to the Psalms of David, for they speak of Christ and celebrate his glory.

2. "The daring impiety of the heretic Paul was manifested in this, that he took as much liberty with these Psalms, whose author is the Holy Spirit, as though they had been the compositions of uninspired men.

3. "The psalmody which he introduced was designed to celebrate his own praise. He appointed women in the church, on the great day of Easter, to sing songs in honour of himself, the hearing of which was adapted to fill the pious mind with horror."*

II. The Mediæval hymnology. From the period at which we have arrived in our inquiries, the subject of psalmody in the time of the Papal apostacy, is, of course, of little account in settling any controversy. As early as the age of Ambrose—who wrote many hymns—and indeed, from the third century, hymns, Greek and Latin, fast multiplied. It was the age of rapid declension in knowledge, in purity, in fidelity to the word of

* Pressly, pp. 164—172.

God. Evils of every kind grew apace; soon reaching their culmination in the rise of the Antichrist.

Passing over many centuries, we come to the middle ages, when we note two facts. The *first*, which we give in the words of the writer of the "Voice of the Christian Life." Speaking of the hymn-writers of this period, he says, "With one exception, all were monks, and the monotonous routine of monastic life seems in their histories to have replaced the endless varieties of discipline by which our Heavenly Father trains His children." "The one exception to the monastic character of mediæval hymn-writers is King Robert the Second of France, author of the touching hymn, in which all his gentle nature seems to speak, 'Veni Sancta Spiritus;' and King Robert had certainly more of the monk than of the king about him. He seems to have been, if ever any man was, made for the cloister, and being forced into the publicity of the throne, he threw as much as possible of the colouring of the convent over his home and his court."* And again, "We need only study the sacred poetry of the middle ages to understand why the Reformation was needed. One painfully expressed fact meets us at the outset. Of Mone's 'Collection of the Latin Hymns of the Middle Ages,' in three volumes, one is filled with hymns to God and the angels; one with hymns to the blessed Virgin Mary; and one with hymns to the saints." The *second* fact is, that the Albigenses and Waldenses—God's faithful witnesses in Southern France, and among the Alps—were psalm-singers. We quote from Dr. M'Master: "In the middle ages, the ages too of moral gloom and terrible superstition, the purest section of the church of God was found in the valleys of Piedmont. Among the Waldenses were found the simplicity of the apostolic order, and the purity of evangelical worship. They sung, ''mid Alpine cliffs,' the Psalms of Scripture. And

---

* "Voice," &c., pp. 167, 168, 200.

long before the Reformation dawned on Europe, they sung them in metre. 'The Albigenses, in 1210, were metre psalm-singers.' In those ages when darkness covered the earth, and gross darkness all other people, the *Vaudois*, as Thuanus, who was their enemy, relates, 'could all read and write. They were acquainted with French so far as was needful for understanding the Bible, and the *singing of Psalms*.' It was required of those who were to be ordained to the ministry along with other scriptures, to commit to memory 'the writings of David.' Numbers of those, who, under the persecution of the Duke of Savoy, A.D. 1686, sought a refuge in the Swiss cantons, three years after, returned under their pastor, *Arnaud*, who was also their martial chief. Having overcome their enemies, and regained their native valleys, 'at the church of Guigon they engaged in worship, sang the 74th Psalm, and their colonel and pastor, *Arnaud*, preached on the 129th Psalm.' The morning-star of the Reformation used them. *Wickliffe* is blamed by some for singing metre psalms. *John Huss*, in the fifteenth, as Wickliffe had done in the fourteenth century, sung the psalms in verse."*

These are very significant facts. Hymns made by monks or monkish men; and by none other so far as the record has reached the intelligent author of the "Voice," &c., while the only witnesses of Christ, in their purity and obscurity, adhered to the singing of psalms. The lesson is an instructive one. We will not forget it.

III. The Reformed period. The Reformation in Germany, led by Luther, did not reject the use of hymns, although it repudiated *en masse*, Mediæval hymns. This same Reformation, however, retained not a few of the outward appliances of the corrupt system which had succeeded it; and in one instance, at least,

* M'Master, p. 71.

approached too nearly the worst heresy of the Papal system.* It was far otherwise with the Reformation in the Western Church: sometimes styled the Zuinglian or Swiss Reformation, with which affiliated the same great movement, in France, Holland, and Britain; and also in some of the German states themselves. We quote again from the " Voice of the Christian Life," &c. " The Reformed Churches of France and French Switzerland seem to have had no literature corresponding to the hymns of Protestant Germany. Did the peculiar form which the Reformation took in France, then, tend to quench the spirit of sacred poetry, or what other causes brought about this result? When we remember that the same absence of an evangelical national hymn literature, springing up spontaneously as a national growth of the Reformation, which characterizes the Reformed Churches of France and French Switzerland, exists also in the sister Church of Scotland, it is impossible not to connect this fact with the similar form which the Reformation took in all these lands. *None of the strictly Calvinistic communities have a hymn-book dating back to the Reformation.* It cannot surely be their doctrine which caused this; many of the best known and most deeply treasured of the more modern hymns of Germany and England have been written by those who receive the doctrines known as Calvinistic. Nor can it proceed from any peculiarity of race, or deficiency in popular love of music and song. French and Scotch national character are too dissimilar to explain the resemblance; whilst France has many national melodies and songs, and Scotland is peculiarly rich in both. Is not the cause then simply the common ideal of external ecclesiastical forms which pervaded all the Churches reformed on the Genevan type? The intervening chapters of church history are, as it were, folded up, as too blotted and marred for

---

* We mean the Doctrine of Consubstantiation held by Luther.

truth to be read to profit in them; and, next to the first chapter in the Acts of the Apostles, was to stand, as the second chapter, the history of the Reformed Churches. Words were to resume their original Bible meaning, *nothing was to be received that could not be traced back to the Divine hand.* Ecclesiastical order was to be such as St. Paul had established or had found established; clearly to be traced, it was believed, in the Acts and Apostolical Epistles. Thus, the Book of Psalms became the hymn-book of the Reformed Churches, adapted to grave and solemn music, in metrical translations whose one aim and glory was to render into measure which could be sung the very words of the old Hebrew Psalms."*

Passing to England, this author proceeds: " The Church of England is, in form, linked to the Mediæval Church by ties far stronger and more numerous than the Lutheran Churches of Germany. The thinking people of England were, after the Marian exiles returned from the Continent, more strongly attracted to the Protestantism of Switzerland and Scotland than to that of Germany. Thus, between Anglicanism and Puritanism, it happened that, until the last century, we cannot be said to have had any national, that is, *any people's hymn-book at all.* Probably no person or community ever felt any enthusiasm either for Sternhold and Hopkins, or Tate and Brady; and although some stray hymns have crept into our modern hymnbooks from earlier days, until the eighteenth century, we had no People's Hymn-book; none, that is, that was placed on cottage tables besides the Bible, and sung when Christians met, and chanted beside the grave. The Wesleys seem to have been the first who gave a People's Hymn-book to England; unless that of Dr. Watts may be called so, published about the beginning of the *eighteenth century.* Not, indeed, that

---

* " Voice," &c., 252—254.

England was silent those two hundred years, or that the sacred chain of holy song was ever altogether broken in our country. We had our 'Te Deum' and 'Magnificat,' and the English Psalms in the music of their own grand and touching prose—a melody as much deeper to our ears than any metrical manufacture of the same, as the morning song of a thrush is, than the notes of a caged bird that has been painfully taught to sing two or three tunes. These were said in village church and quiet home, making rich melody in the heart, and pealed through the old cathedrals to choral chant, in a language 'understood of all the people.' The Prayer-book, with all its musical flow of choice words, floating down on its clear stream of pure English, the song and prayer of the true church of all ages, and the English Psalter—this was the hymn-book of half our people; while, in many a Puritan congregation, the heroic purposes of the heart, the individuality of Puritan religion, which made every hymn sung as by each worshipper alone 'to God,' must have breathed poetry into any verses, and fused them, by inward fire, into a music no external polish could ever give. With the eighteenth century, however, the history of English hymn-books must begin."* And of Scotland we need not speak. Her Reformers neither made hymns nor sung them.

Let us now sum up the history of psalmody, and thus turn the objector's argument against himself. 1. The "psalms, hymns, and spiritual songs" of the Bible passed over to the New Testament Church. 2. There is not a shadow of historical evidence that any other hymns were sung in apostolic times in the worship of God. 3. Some heretics did, at an early period, make and use hymns; but these earliest of human composures have disappeared, leaving behind them only the fact that they once existed; or, at most, a few

* "Voice," &c., 255, 256, 259.

waifs which cannot be recognized or allotted to time and space. 4. The first known orthodox hymn-writer lived at the close of the second century, and there is no evidence that the single hymn which he composed was ever sung in God's worship. 5. Opposition was made at a later period to the introduction of human compositions, while the psalms of the Bible were held in the highest estimation, and were sung both in the East and in the West. 6. During the middle ages, the Waldenses sang the psalms: hymns were made by monks, and sung in the Popish communion. 7. At the Reformation the psalms exclusively were used in worship in the "strictly Calvinistic churches." The Lutheran churches, which retained some of the trappings of Popery, retaining also the use of hymns. 8. The practice of Calvinistic churches was based upon the principle, that the Bible is the only rule in worship. 9. The Church of England was then almost exclusively a psalm-singing church. 10. No hymn-book was found in the Western Reformed Churches until something more than a century ago. Hence, 11. The Scripture Psalms were ever sung in God's worship in the purest days and parts of the church—in the Apostles' days, among the Waldenses, and in the most scriptural of the Reformed Churches.

Whatever assistance the cause of hymn-singing may derive from the occasional use of hymns in times, either ancient or modern, when religion had begun to decline, or from their use among the followers of Antichrist, we cheerfully allow it; but we do claim, that in using exclusively the Bible Psalms, we follow the "footsteps of the flock."

IV. The advocates of these other songs and hymns argue from analogy: we may compose and offer our own prayers, why not hymns also? Dr. Pressly thus satisfactorily disposes of this argument: " However plausible this argument may appear at first view, a little examination may satisfy the honest inquirer after truth, that it is entirely fallacious. The things which are compared are dissimilar, and, consequently, the reasoning is inconclusive. Prayer and praise agree in one particular, and that is, they are both ordinances of religious worship. But in almost every thing else they differ. And, therefore, it is a pure assumption to say, that because we may employ our own language in prayer, therefore it is proper to compose in our own language our songs of praise to God. Not only are these religious exercises different in their nature, but, that God himself regards them in a different light, is evident from the fact, that He has made provision for His church in the one case, which He has not in the other. But that the reader may see more satisfactorily the difference between these Divine ordinances, and the absolute necessity for provision in the one case, which is not necessary in the other; and, consequently, the fallacy of the conclusion which is drawn by those who reason from the one ordinance to the other; let us notice a little more in detail, some particulars in which they differ.

1. "In prayer we come to God to ask for those things which we need; but in praise we ascribe to Him the glory which is due unto His name. As our situation and circumstances are ever varying, our wants are very different at one time, from what they are at another. Our petitions must, consequently, be framed in accordance with our wants. But God is unchangeable, and His praise is always the same. That glory which is proper to be ascribed to His name, at one time, will always be proper. No matter what may be our situation; whether we may be in prosperity or in adversity; whether we may be the subjects of joy or of sorrow, still God is to be praised for what He is in Himself, and for the exhibitions of His glory which He has made in the works of creation, of providence, and of redemption. And what ascriptions of glory are due to Him, the Spirit of God has declared in those

psalms and hymns and songs, which are the productions of His infinite wisdom.

2 "In social prayer, one leads in the exercise, while others follow and unite with him in presenting their supplications before the throne of grace; but, in praise, all simultaneously lift up their voices together in extolling the name of God. And hence it results, that in the exercise of praise, a written form is absolutely necessary, while in prayer, such form is unnecessary. And hence, as our songs of praise assume a character of permanency, which does not belong to our prayers, we can see an important and obvious reason, why provision should be made for our assistance in the performance of the one duty, which was not considered necessary in the other. And in connexion with this consideration, I remark—

3. "That since, in singing God's praise, a written form is necessary, there is provided for the church, in the word of God, a Book of Psalms, while there is no Book of Prayers. This is a fact which deserves special attention. The infinitely wise God, does nothing in vain, and never works without design. From every part of the word of God we learn that it is our duty, both to pray to Him and to sing praises to His name. And while the duty in both cases is perfectly plain, it is no less evident, that God has made provision with regard to the performance of the one duty, which He has not thought proper to make with reference to the other. Not only are we commanded to sing psalms, but a Book of Psalms which contains the songs of the Spirit of purity, of love, and of grace, is provided for our use. Men may say, that 'as we use our own language in prayer, so may we in praise;' but the fact that God has Himself provided for us a Book of Psalms, while He has given us no Book of Prayers, rebukes the unwarranted assertion. And from the provision already made for us by Him who knows the glory due to Himself, there is no need for us to prepare songs of praise, unless we are disposed to adopt the presump-

tuous principle, that we are more competent to decide what is proper to be employed in praising God, than He himself who is the object of praise. But in relation to prayer, the case is entirely different. While it is plainly our duty to pray, He with whom is the residue of the Spirit, has not thought proper to provide for us a collection of prayers. And consequently, in complying with the divine command—'In every thing by prayer and supplication, with thanksgiving, let your requests be made known unto God'—we must, from the necessity of the case, express our requests in our own language. The reader can, therefore, have no difficulty in perceiving that the cases are dissimilar, and consequently, that it is by no means a legitimate conclusion, that, as we may use our own language in prayer, so may we in praise. But still further—

4. "Our Lord taught His disciples to pray, and gave them an admirable form of prayer, with reference to which He has said, 'After this manner pray ye.'

"But He gave His disciples no divine song, as a model of praise, according to which they were to compose their songs, with a direction, as in the case of prayer, to sing after this manner. And why, with reverence I would ask, did not the great prophet of the church, furnish in the New Testament a book of sacred hymns, or direct some one of His Apostles to perform this service? The only rational answer which can be given to this inquiry, is, that He did not consider it necessary. He had already raised up a sweet Psalmist of Israel, whom He had qualified for the work, and by whom He had provided for His church, such a collection of psalms, and hymns, and songs, as to His infinite wisdom and goodness seemed proper.

"And with regard to the difference between these two religious duties, I observe once more—

5. "That as provision has been made in the case of praise, which has not been made with regard to prayer, so there is a promise of divine help in the performance

of the duty of prayer, which is not given in relation to praise. It is graciously promised by Him who is the hearer of prayer—'I will pour upon the house of David, and upon the inhabitants of Jerusalem, the Spirit of grace and of supplications.' (Zech. xii. 10.) And as the Christian needs assistance in performing the duty of prayer, for which provision has not yet been made, we find it written—'The Spirit also helpeth our infirmities; for we know not what we should pray for as we ought; but the Spirit itself maketh intercession for us with groanings which cannot be uttered.' (Rom. viii. 26.) Here then we see, that the God of grace, who knows what the Christian needs, has graciously promised divine assistance to direct us in the expression of our requests in prayer—'We know not what to pray for as we ought; but the Spirit helpeth our infirmities.' We have no Book of Prayers, in the use of which we may make our requests known unto God; but we have the promise of the aid of the Spirit of grace and of supplications, to help our infirmities, and to instruct us how to pray. But there is no promise in all the New Testament, of the aid of the Holy Spirit, as the Spirit of psalmody, *to aid us in preparing our songs of praise*. He, in whom are hid all the treasures of wisdom and knowledge, did not think proper to raise up, under the gospel dispensation, a sweet Psalmist of Israel, to provide for the church a system of songs, as He had formerly done; nor did He commission any of His Apostles to perform the service; nor did He promise to send His Spirit in any subsequent age, to qualify any man for the execution of a work of such importance. And why not? The only satisfactory answer which can be given, is that such a service was unnecessary, since it had already been performed.

"It is then quite manifest, not only that prayer and praise are religious duties, which are different in their nature, but that God himself regards them as so different that, in His infinite wisdom, He has thought proper to make that provision for the use of His church in the one case, which He has not in the other. It is no valid objection to our reasoning to say, that some of the psalms are termed prayers; that the language of prayer is employed throughout the psalms; and that in prayer we ascribe praise to God. All this may be true. In these particulars, and in others which might be mentioned, there may be a coincidence between these two exercises of religious worship. But still it remains true, that prayer and praise are not only two different ordinances, but that God regards them as different, and has made provision to aid us in the performance of the duty of praise, which he has not furnished for our assistance in prayer. And, consequently, to say that, since it is proper in prayer to use our own language, therefore it is right to do the same in singing God's praise, is to reason after the manner of men, but not in accordance with the wisdom of God."*

V. The right to make and use "hymns" is claimed to be a part of our Christian liberty: and in this connexion we are reminded of the character of the New Testament dispensation as one of greater light, freeness, and enlargement, than the old; and perhaps it may be suggested, likewise, that such as decline to use "hymns" are rather narrow-minded and illiberal.

But what is the Christian liberty of the New Testament dispensation? Most certainly it is not a liberty to form our doctrinal belief, or rules of life, or religious observances, irrespective of the Word and authority of Christ. It consists in part—the part which alone can have any relation to the issue before us—in our liberation from the bondage of the Mosaic ritual and ceremonial law. This was a burdensome service. But was it ever a "bondage" to sing the psalms of inspiration? to hold fellowship with the Most High in the exercise of praise, in the very thoughts and expressions which

* Pressly on Psalmody, pp. 120—125.

He himself had furnished? It never was—none will dare to say so—and it is not now. This argument is a most decided example of that kind of fallacious reasoning which is styled "begging the question." The issue before us is, "Have we liberty to make and sing in the worship of God, songs other than those of the Bible?" Yes—say these reasoners—we have this liberty,—because—we have this liberty! We answer, this is the very issue on which we are brought into conflict; and you do not prove your position by *asserting* it, however often and confidently.

VI. It is said that songs composed by uninspired men, may be read with edification, and even uttered in musical, instead of mere speaking tones, by an individual, and why not use them in religious worship? We are not disposed to deny the premises here affirmed. We do not go so far as to maintain that the human voice may not be used in singing, as well as in reading, other songs than those in which God is formally worshipped. But there must be, and is, a wide difference between the singing of songs for recreation, or even as an expression of our own emotions whether sad or joyful, and the employment of songs in the solemn and devout prescribed worship of God. There is an *ordinance* of praise, which this reasoning leaves entirely out of view. Any one who is capable may write a religious essay, He may read it in the hearing of others. Any one may speak on religious topics in social intercourse. But there is still the *ordinance* of preaching, and the institution of the ministry, established and guarded by the will of Christ. Nor is every utterance of gospel truth by a Christian minister, the formal preaching of the Word. So, there is an institution of government and discipline in the house of God; and yet, it is competent to every Christian to admonish and warn his erring brother. Again, every act that we perform in our daily avocations should be done to the "glory of God;" and yet there are exercises properly and formally devotional. Every day should the Christian live unto Christ, yet is there one day in seven set apart, specially, for religious worship. As we peruse the Bible, and so in reading Christian biography, we may read many prayers, and be instructed and quickened by them, but there is still an *ordinance* of prayer. Any one may, under certain circumstances put into another's hand, a morsel of bread and a cup of wine, but there is, notwithstanding, the *ordinance* of the Lord's Supper. We may make pictures—these may represent scenes of deep religious interest—the sufferings of the martyrs, the trials of the persecuted, or other events calculated to stir up devout recollections, or grateful emotions : we may have them in our dwellings, we may look upon them; and be edified as we do so.

Now, would we listen to one who would attempt to demonstrate that there is no ministry, no church discipline, no holyday, no sacrament of the supper, no formal prayer, by insisting upon the right, or the duty of private Christians to give utterance to the truths of the gospel, to rebuke the sinner, to lead a holy life, " to do all in the name of the Lord Jesus," to feed the hungry and minister to the sick, to read the prayers offered by the saints in their day? Or, from the lawful use of paintings in our dwellings, will any one of *us* argue—we know who do thus argue—that these and similar appliances, may be introduced into our places of worship as " aids to devotion?" So, in answer to this argument, we say, there is an ordinance of praise, and when we inquire of the word of God, how this ordinance is to be observed, we find not only that it is a scripture ordinance, but also that provision has been made for its observance—and, as we shall see hereafter, for wise reasons—in a Book of Psalms, itself sufficient as a manual of praise. We must not confound, as this argument does, the reading,* or even the singing of

* Erskine's Gospel Sonnets are excellent reading: but were never meant for "hymns," or used in worship.

songs, however good, and the formal celebration in acts of worship, of God's high praises.

But what is the ordinance of praise? Does it consist merely in the use of musical instead of reading tones? And can there be so much difference between these two modes of uttering the same sentiments, as that the one is allowable, and the other not? This is a very subtle form of the general argument which we have just considered. And we remark—(1.) That the same kind of reasoning would be equally available, as we have seen, to confound other religious acts and ordinances with the doings of every day, or of the Christian life. (2.) It is not the mere use of singing tones, but the design of the act, and its circumstances, which we are here to consider, just as we do in reference to baptism, the Lord's supper, and laying on of hands in the act of ordination. Are we engaged in celebrating God's praise in song, according to His appointment, and in circumstances to which that appointment relates? If so, we must have regard to something more than the tones merely in which we utter our praises. We must take with us the entire institution of praise as a part of the prescribed order of worship. Hence, (3.) It is most important to remember that we have a book, provided by Him whose name we magnify in song, and appointed for this very end; and no *command* or *promise* regarding another. Had we a Book of Prayers in the Scriptures—were we commanded to use this—were there no precept enjoining the use of any prayers not contained in this book—were there no promises of help in making prayers, the whole ordinance of prayer would be comprehended within this inspired liturgy, with the appropriate and prescribed restrictions, seasons, &c. We have no such prayer-book; but we have a hymn, or psalm book—similar in position, in reference to the ordinance of praise, as our supposed inspired prayer-book to that of prayer. Hence, we ought to infer that, in singing praises, this alone is to be used; whatever other uses we may lawfully make of song. (4.) If there were no difference between reading and singing, we might omit the singing entirely, and only *read* psalms and hymns! would this be the *ordinance* of praise? (5.) God has linked singing of psalms to the ordinance of praise, and we should not cavil about it, as if there were no material difference. (6.) While we do not undertake to assign *the* reasons for this divine ordinance, we may be at liberty to say, that song is a powerful medium of propagating sympathy, as well as of awakening it; and, again, that there are proofs abundant, arising chiefly from the peculiar power of songs over the faith, &c., of those that use them in their devotions, that it was not unbecoming the divine wisdom to make this restriction.

VII. It has been said, that inasmuch as the minister of Christ uses his own words in his public ministry, and may even quote a hymn, we may do so likewise in singing praise: and this for the reason that preaching is a part of public worship. To this, it is enough in this place to reply, that there is a vast difference between addresses made *to God* in song, and an address made to an assembled congregation; the preacher does not preach to the Most High—he speaks to the people before him. He who would confound these under the general name of "worship" has yet to learn the proper nature of each part of our social religious exercises.

VIII. An argument is taken from the fact, that men have now the "gift of song," implying, it is said, that they may use it in providing songs for the church's use in her devotions. To this we reply: (1.) The gift of song existed under the Old Testament, and yet none, unless such as were specially inspired of God, were employed in composing songs for purposes of devotion. (2.) We hear nothing of any poet in the apostolic church undertaking to make hymns; not one hymn can be traced to the days of the Apostles: and yet there were some, no doubt, who could have written in metre.

Paul could, we are quite confident; yet we have no hint of any attempt on his part to make a hymn-book. (3.) If there be any validity in this argument, it takes a wide sweep. If the possession of the gift confers the *right* to use it in making songs for the church, who can refuse to adopt and sing *any given* hymn: the poet can claim a divine sanction—authority direct from heaven—and who dare repudiate any of his works? (4.) The church, in her members, has the gift of speech! Is every one that can speak entitled to claim the office of the ministry? It is not enough to have the gift: there must be a warrant to use it for this specific purpose in the house of God. And so of song. Let those who have the gift show us a Scripture warrant—we have seen that they cannot—to prepare us songs other than those of the Bible. (5.) There is still among men, and some of them Christians, the gifts of sculpture, &c.: must we employ them to provide us statues and ornaments for our churches? (6.) This is, again, a "begging of the question." We deny the right to use this gift *for this particular purpose.* To establish this right, they must furnish us with better authority than the mere possession of the gift.

IX. It is affirmed that godly men have favoured the use of hymns—have composed and sung them during their lives—have been edified by them—and have died without experiencing any scruples upon this subject.

The facts asserted in this argument we may admit. Devout men have so thought, and so acted; but the conclusion we utterly repudiate. To receive all that even excellent men have held, would make strange work in the church. Many good men have lived in the belief of doctrines more or less erroneous, and have retained their errors to the last. Should we adopt these errors, or even tolerate them? Good men have differed in relation to important matters of practice, as well as of faith. Some have been Presbyterians, some Episcopalians, some Independents. The Jansenists—and some of these were pious men—held many of the errors of the Popish system, particularly the Papal supremacy. What kind of a church that would be, which should attempt to combine in one system, upon the authority of the pious and devout, these heterogeneous, and often positively inconsistent principles, can scarcely be imagined—certainly, it could not be described. We would have a parity of the ministry *and* diocesan bishops! A prayer-book, *and* no prayer-book! government by sessions, by presbyteries, &c., *and* by the people, presbyters being excluded! The Pope acknowledged, *and* at the same time renounced as the Antichrist! To say nothing of a *profession* in the same church of conflicting opinions on important matters of faith. And as to the edification of good men by the use of such songs, it is not impossible that the truths which they may contain may be employed for this end by the Spirit of God, even when the songs themselves are improperly used. Of this we have no need to judge.

The truth is, in this whole matter, men are no rule of faith or of duty. "To the law, and to the testimony." The Word of God alone is a "lamp unto the feet, a light unto the path." Men—good men—owing to the imperfection of human knowledge, may build upon the one foundation, "wood, hay, and stubble," and still be saved, while their works shall be burned up (1 Cor. iii. 11—14); but surely we are not bound, or even warranted, to copy their errors—to appropriate their "wood, hay, and stubble!" The safe rule is that which the Spirit furnishes, speaking by the great Apostle, "Be ye followers of me, even as I am of Christ." (1 Cor. xi. 1)

X. It has been supposed, and urged, that the singing of the Psalms of Scripture, in a New Testament sense, "with our hearts and minds full of the New Testament commentary," is somehow a warrant for the making and using of hymns: and this upon the principle that "It cannot be wrong to express in words, in the worship of God, what it is right to conceive in thought." It has also been stated, in this connexion, that "the most rigid advocates of an Old Testament Psalmody first comment, and at the close of his commentary, the minister counsels the people to sing as he has expounded!" And it is added, "It comes to this, that we must choose between a prose commentary which can neither be remembered nor sung, and a metrical comment, which all may hold with their hands, and look upon with their eyes, and render vocal with their tongues."

On this very singular argument for hymns we remark—(1.) If we mistake not, the design of all comment is to ascertain and trace the *true* meaning of the Scriptures, whether Old Testament or New. (2.) We were not aware that the minister who expounds the Word of God, imposes an *obligation* upon his hearers, either to read or to sing the words of the Bible "as he has expounded." We had imagined that expositors, whether writing or speaking, were "helps," and not "lords of the faith" of the hearer. (3.) If the psalms are correctly expounded, the worshipper is aided in singing them "with the spirit and with the understanding;" if incorrectly, he is not only at liberty to reject the comment, but bound to do so. (4.) If this argument is worth anything for the purpose for which it is adduced, it is equally available to a much greater extent; for it might as well be said, that the hearer is bound to *read* his Bible—any part of it—with the minister's comment in his mind and heart, as to sing a psalm as it is expounded. (5.) It seems to be taken for granted here, that New Testament truth is not *in* the psalm, but is merely put into the commentary; for, certainly, if this truth be there already, it can do no harm, and may do much good, to have the fact clearly set forth, as we are about to sing. (6.) If it be right to fix, by a metrical version, prepared as a paraphrase and not a translation, the meaning of a psalm, and use this instead of the psalm itself, why not apply this rule to the whole Bible, and re-write *it*, in the form of a paraphrase, so that no comments will be needed, and then put this into the "hands" of the people as an infallible exposition? Hence—(7.) The concluding statement of this argument is inconsistent with true Protestantism; for it advocates this very thing—the substitution of our own words as a commentary for the words of the Bible itself, in the exercise of praise. (8.) The whole argument, if it has any force at all, is valid only against *explaining* the psalms, and if so, against explaining any part of the Bible. We now proceed—

II. *To adduce some arguments against the use of uninspired hymns in the church's worship, whether domestic, social, or public.* It can hardly be necessary to remark, that we do not object to the expression of Scripture truth in rhythmical forms. An author may make "Gospel Sonnets," as well as "sermons." The only question is, regarding the use of them in the worship of God. Against this we argue. And,

I. The praises of God were celebrated in song, for many centuries under the Old Testament economy, but only in inspired songs. We have already seen, in one of our quotations from the pen of Dr. Pressly, that the church in the patriarchal age seems, so far as we have any light at all upon this subject, to have conducted the worship of God without the use of song. Neither the Bible, nor tradition, gives any other evidence. That the poetical faculty was entirely wanting, is extremely improbable. Yet none ever attempted, until inspired of God, to provide songs to be used in religious exercises. Still more. In after ages God was praised in song; but only in song as indited by the Holy Ghost. None ventured to obtrude their own compositions upon the people of God as the matter of their praise. Hence, in times subsequent to David and Asaph, we find Hezekiah and Judah, in the great reformation accomplished in the reign of that good king, employing none other than the psalms already furnished. (2 Chron. xxix. 30.) And so throughout the entire Old Testament dispensation. Poets there were, unquestionably; and yet, no psalms or hymns were ever introduced into God's worship except inspired psalms and hymns; none at all, after the canon of Old Testament Scripture had been completed. This is an instructive and admonitory fact; to be met only by the clearest and most unquestionable warrant in the New Testament: such a warrant as we have already seen cannot be adduced.

II. There is no authority by which we are, or can be called upon, to sing uninspired hymns. It needs no argument to show that the poet himself cannot make this demand upon us. We may refuse to sing his songs, and do no dishonour to God. Nor can the minister by reading from his place such songs, impose the obligation upon his fellow-worshippers to sing them. His audience may sit in silence and decline to respond to his call, which they cannot do, without sin, if able to sing, when called upon to unite in praising God in the "psalms and hymns and spiritual songs" of the Scriptures, upon which He has impressed the sanction of His own authority, any more than they can refuse to read His word, or wait upon the ministry which He has appointed. We might have in our possession any hymn-book, for half a century, unopened, confining ourselves to the Psalms of the Bible, and be guiltless before God: which we could not do if it had His authority and sanction as containing the matter in which He is to be praised in song. Nor has the church any authority to make and enforce the reception and use of a hymn-book. For even in those churches in which hymn-books have been authorized in modern times— there was no such true church until of late—no scruples hinder the most severe criticisms upon the very hymns which have received the very highest sanction —criticisms affecting, not merely the poetry and the rhyme, but the very matter and entire character of the hymn.* And it is not impossible but that the whole book might be thus handled by various critics, each adducing objections against such songs as might offend his views or his tastes. Hence, we are compelled to conclude that even those who have no difficulty in conscience as to the use of uninspired compositions, are conscious that the church has not been commissioned to prepare a book of hymns—that when the task has been undertaken, the book is still destitute of any authority that can claim its devout and conscientious reception and use.

But we go farther. If these hymns have no authorized place in God's worship; if they are destitute of His high sanction, they can be regarded in no other light than as "will-worship;" that is, worship of man' device, and, hence, not only unprofitable, but unacceptable; not only unacceptable, but offensive in God's sight, and so to be most carefully eschewed. Thus, as we have seen, in our history of psalmody, our reforming fathers thought. They rejected, on this principle, all matter of praise in song, but that which they found prescribed and ordered of God.

III. The employment of human compositions in the worship of God, does, in fact, set aside, at least for the time, the Psalms of the Bible. The advocates of hymns are not entirely agreed as to the propriety of using the Scripture Psalms at all. Some go so far as to deny them any rightful place in New Testament worship. The great majority, however, admit that they *may* be used, and that too, as a manual of praise, which He who is King in Zion, has provided and appointed. Hence, they are rather disposed, in most cases, to resent the imputation that they exclude God's Psalms from His own house, and assert that they claim no more than the right to sing other songs by times. On this we remark, (1.) That it suggests the inquiry,

---

* Instances of this will be given in the sequel.

whether they allow to the Psalms of the Bible a place of higher authority, than they do to their own writings? Do they sing them because they are God's, and appointed by Him, or solely on the ground that they are *selected by the worshipper for this purpose*—or, it may be allowed by church authority? If they can sing, or omit to sing them, as they determine at the time, alternating them with " hymns," it would appear to be quite clear that there can be no regard to God's appointment at all; or, at least that that appointment is liable to be overruled, at any time, by the choice of the worshipper. This is the only fair conclusion from the premises; and yet we are far from affirming that all who thus act, do deliberately subject a Divine appointment to the taste, or judgment, or caprice of the worshipper: *but they act as if they did.* (2.) Is it not evident—provided the Bible Psalms have a sanction which cannot be claimed for songs of man's composing, that the use of these songs in God's worship, *at any given time,* is derogatory to this authority and sanction? If the Most High has appointed the Psalms to be sung in His praise, and has fixed the seal of His appointment to no other hymns or songs—and this we have already shown —then, does it not follow, that in mingling a hymn in our devotions, we do, for the time, set aside an appointment of God, and this on the ground, expressed or implied, that we have found something better; for this occasion at least? Should we use, five times out of six, the Psalms of the Bible, we would really exclude them from their appointed place by the substitution of something else for the sixth service of song: for, if these psalms be provided for our use, as God's ordained matter of praise, it is not merely when we *choose* to use them that the command bears upon us, but all the time. (3.) The inevitable conclusion is, that to mingle mere human hymns with the " Psalms," is nothing less than to exclude the latter from the position they are entitled, as given of God, to occupy—is to make a Divine appointment to depend upon our own will. If we may set them aside for one time, we may, for the same reasons, and, on no higher authority, set them aside entirely and for ever.

IV. Hymns, such as we oppose, are *sectarian*. Every hymn-singing denomination has its own hymn-book. There is a Methodist hymn-book, a Baptist hymn-book, a Congregational hymn-book, or books, a Presbyterian hymn-book, or books, a Cumberland Presbyterian hymn-book, a Universalist hymn-book, &c., &c. This is a kind of necessity; acknowledged by high authority to be so. We refer to the Biblical Repertory (vol. xviii. p. 505)—"The Psalmody of the Christian assembly has generally partaken largely of those characteristics of thought and expression, which arise from the circumstances of the people. In a divided state of the Church, when the different denominations are zealous for their respective forms of doctrine and worship, the lyric poetry becomes strongly argumentative and polemical: addresses men rather than God; and is employed to defend and inculcate theology, and to confirm the attachment of the people to their peculiar articles of faith. Hence each sect has its psalmody. Both policy and conscience are deemed to require the hymns to coincide in sentiment throughout with the creed of the sect. And these doctrines are not only stated in poetical language, or language professedly poetical, and dwelt upon in a strain of devout meditation, but are frequently inculcated in a sort of metrical argument, and appeal to persons not supposed to believe them."

In opposition to all this sectarian perversion of this part of God's worship, the advocates of the exclusive use of the Scripture Psalms hold large minded and catholic views. That the church may become one in her visible organization, and in worship, some at least of their hymn-books *must* be sacrificed. They cannot *all* remain. Let them all be discarded, that the one and sufficient Book of Psalms furnished by our Saviour himself, through the inspiring influences of His Spirit, may be alone made use of by all His people, in the holy exercise of praise. The *coming* unity of the church will abolish these uninspired hymn-books, or, at least, exclude them from the sacred worship of God.

V. It has been found impracticable—especially in the more enlightened and orthodox denominations—to frame a hymn-book universally acceptable, and of a permanent character. Change, change, change, has been written and re-written upon these efforts to get better songs for Christian worship than those of the Bible. We might here, very properly allude, once more, to the fact that every denomination has its peculiar system of hymns. Every new schism produces some change in the songs sung in religious exercises. Every new phase of doctrine, particularly when it puts on a visible form as the exciting cause and shibboleth of a new ecclesiastical organization, makes its appearance in the shape of new hymns; destined themselves to illustrate, in turn, the inherent—and we believe insuperable—difficulty in the way of securing entire unanimity. In this connexion, we present, as quoted by Mr. Sommerville, some testimonies in regard to the estimation in which the majority of existing hymns is held by some, at least, who do not confine themselves to the use of Scripture Psalms. "A 'Layman' in the *New York Independent*, Feb. 23, 1854, says—' We have some two thousand pieces which are called Psalms or Hymns. Perhaps two hundred of them may pass for odes or lyrics suitable for singing. Fifty more might possibly be selected by an expert.' The *Boston Congregationalist*, Feb. 15, 1853, has the following:—' Professor B. B. Edwards believed that two or three hundred Psalms or Hymns would include all which are of sterling value for the sanctuary.' Unquestionably he was right. The popular demand for new and more numerous hymns, it cannot be denied, arises in part from the wide dissatisfaction with a large number of those with which our hymn-books are filled. Let us have fewer and choicer. Let them be truly sacred lyrics, and not feeble prose, measured and amputated to the proper length, and afterwards still further mangled, at the mercy of men who wonder that David (or rather the Holy Ghost, who spake by him) 'had not sufficient native sense to have composed his psalms in proper metres, ready at once to be cantered through 'De Fleury, or paced through State street.' The *Glasgow Examiner* for Sept. 18, 1852, thus remarks upon the 'Hymn-book of the U. P. Church:' 'The collections contain a great many beautiful effusions of sanctified genius, and not a few *very trashy productions.*'"

The last hymn-book of the Presbyterian Church (Old School) furnishes an example in proof of our statement deserving of especial notice. This book is the result of a *second* and laborious attempt to prepare a proper hymn-book. The first, which was compiled by a very able committee of the Assembly, and by the labours of a number of years, and which was long sung, was an *acknowledged* failure. The committee to whom was entrusted, in 1838, the task of revising it, pronounced in their report to the Assembly the following judgment upon its demerits: "On a critical examination, they found many hymns deficient in literary merit, some incorrect in doctrine, and many altogether unsuitable for the sanctuary as songs of praise, for want of suitable sentiments, although not incorrect in doctrine or deficient in literary merit."*

But did this committee, whose report, and a new book, which they had compiled, were adopted in 1840, succeed any better in satisfying the whole body? The Biblical Repertory, conducted by the Professors of the Theological Seminary at Princeton, says: "We are free to confess that there are many things in the book laid before the Assembly which we think ought not to

---

* Spirit of the Nineteenth Century, vol. ii. 582.

be there; hymns which we consider unsuitable for the worship of God. Some of them are mere sentimental effusions; some objectionable for the lightness of their measure, and others for their want of all poetic excellence." Others agreed with the Repertory; and just now a spirit of dissatisfaction with their hymns begins to make itself manifest in influential quarters. The "Southern Presbyterian," a paper connected with that denomination, referring to a difficulty which has arisen out of a late discovery that one hymn occurs twice in the book, says: "It is not enough to 'remove duplicate hymns;' those must be removed which are *unpoetical* and lacking in *lyrical* merit.' It thinks some of the hymns would do very well as 'doctrinal treatises, spiritual maxims, practical lessons, didactic essays, doctrinal argumentations and defences, very sensible, but very sedate and *angular* moralizings in verse.' Hence some of these 'are neither read nor sung—not sung, because they are not *fit for the purpose;* and not read, because people do not *now* go to the hymn-book when they feel like reading.' And then proceeds thus: 'But it may be asked, What harm do those pieces in the book? We reply, they encumber it; they are in the way when one is looking for hymns that *are* hymns; they increase the price, whilst they add nothing to the value of the volume. We say nothing about the credit they do us, or fail to do us, as a denomination *making some pretensions to taste in poetry*, as in other things. This is a tender subject, and we do not wish to give offence. Wonder if Dr. Dewey had not been recently looking over some of these pieces, when he asked with so pompous, triumphant emphasis, 'What poem has Calvinism written?'"

A "greatly respected correspondent" of the *Presbyterian* of this city, and "who has given the subject," we use the words of the editor, "much consideration," thus writes of the hymnology of the times, making no exceptions in regard to any particular system: "Our hymnology is far enough from perfection. It has grave defects and blemishes. It needs emending and purging. It does not recognise and carry out, as a distinctive and controlling principle, this—that song, in the devotions of the family and the church, is truly a service of worship. It abounds with hymns addressed to creatures, sinners, saints, angels, the living and the dead. These hymns are not the impassioned cry of an adoring soul, calling on all things to praise and magnify the Lord. That is of the very essence of worship. But they reason, exhort, expostulate, promise, threaten; they moralize, soliloquize—sometimes eulogize. They sing to frail, sinful, dying men—not to the great and holy God. And as our books liberally provide such compositions, ministers and people use them, and have used them, until the sense of their incongruity with the idea and fact of worship is almost or quite effaced."*

Nor is there universal acquiescence in the common opinion among such as use hymns, of the excellency of Watts' "Imitations." Dr. R. J. Breckenridge, a very competent judge, uses this language regarding it: " We freely confess that, for ourselves, we consider the Paraphrase of the Psalms, by Dr. Watts, the most defective part of our psalmody; and only more and more marvel that such a miserable attempt should have acquired so much reputation."† Dr. Junkin, who holds a high position in the same body—Old School Presbyterian—thus characterizes this attempt to improve the Psalms of the Bible: " Dr. Watts has attempted, professedly, to *improve* upon the sentiment, the very matter, and the order, and by various omissions and additions, to fit the Psalms for Christian worship. This is unfair. If Pope had taken the same license with the poems of Homer, all the amateurs of Greek poetry in the world would have cried—shame on the presumptuous intruder! But it is a pious and zealous Christian divine who has

---

* S. D., in the Presbyterian, Nov. 20th, 1858.
† Spirit of the Nineteenth Century, vol. ii. 586.

taken this liberty with the songs of Zion, and almost the whole church acquiesces in it. What would we think of the French poet who, proposing to enrich French literature with a versification of the masterpiece of the English muse, should mangle and transpose the torn limbs of the Paradise Lost, until Milton himself might meet his first-born on the highway and not recognise it? And must this literary butchery be tolerated, because, forsooth, the victim is the inspired Psalmist? Why should the Heaven-taught bard be misrepresented thus? Let us rather have the songs of inspiration as God inspired them, and as nearly as is possible, and consistent with the laws of English versification. God's order of thought is doubtless the best for his church. If any one think he can write better spiritual songs than the sweet singer of Israel, let him do it; but let him not dress the savoury meat which God hath prepared, until all the substance and savour are gone, and then present it to us as an imitation of David's Psalms."*

Thus the efforts of one of the most intelligent, and orthodox, and literary denominations in this country, have signally failed to procure a hymn-book on whose merits they can agree.† They may try it again; but only to subject themselves to another mortifying failure. Among an ignorant people, or people of lax doctrinal views, it may be possible to secure a more general acquiescence in a volume of hymns. But this does not

---

* Lectures on the Prophecies, by George Junkin, D.D., pp. 231, 233.

† The new hymn-book, we might have said above, was severely criticised on the floor of the Assembly, by which it was adopted. The chairman of the committee, somewhat disturbed by the unfavourable remarks upon the book, at length rose, and said, in substance, that he could sympathize with a good deal that had been said; for after revising each hymn, time after time — in all, some six or seven times, he had thought it " the meanest book he had ever seen,"—adding, with a smile, " of course, I think better of it now."

weaken—it rather strengthens the argument against hymns, derived from the apparent impossibility of attaining this in an educated and inquiring community.

Now, it is certainly not unreasonable that we should demand of these churches that they suit themselves in a book of hymns, before they ask us to join them in the singing of hymns. Indeed, with what propriety—we had almost said, with what decency—can they call upon us to unite with them in laying aside, even in part, if there were no more, the Book of Psalms in a literal rendering, and in the adoption of hymns in our devotions, while they are so far from being satisfied with their new psalmody? We have a book which has stood the test of thousands of years; which, as we have seen, has instructed, edified, and cheered hosts of the saints of God, living and dying; and with which we are fully satisfied.* It is rather too much to ask us to desert the stable position we now occupy, and to enter upon seas of uncertainity—to subject ourselves to similar harassing toils in the hitherto vain pursuit of unity and uniformity in singing hymns of human composition—particularly as we have in the psalms which the Most High has graciously provided us, ample matter for the celebration of His praises.

VI. The advocacy of hymn-singing has led to the adoption and utterance of sentiments which strike at the very fundamentals of Christianity. We begin with Dr. Watts, who "imitated" the Psalms of the Bible, and also prepared many of the hymns now in use. This favourite poet and hymn-writer allowed himself to speak of the Psalms of Scripture in the following terms: "Some of them are *almost opposite* to the spirit of the gospel; hence, it comes to pass, that when spiritual affections are excited within us, and our souls are raised a little above this earth in the beginning of a psalm, we are *checked on a sudden in our ascent towards heaven*, by

---

* Of the version used in our churches, we have something to say in the sequel.

some expressions that are fit only to be sung in *the worldly sanctuary*. When we are just entering into an evangelical frame, the very next *line* which the clerk parcels out to us, hath something in it so *extremely Jewish and cloudy*, that *it darkens our sight of God the Saviour*. Thus, by keeping too close to David in the house of God, *the vail of Moses is thrown over our hearts*. While we are kindling into divine love, some *dreadful curse* against men is proposed to our lips; *as*, Ps. lxix. 26—28, which is *so contrary* to the new commandment of loving our enemies. *Some sentences* of the Psalmist may compose our spirits to seriousness, but we meet with a following line, that *breaks off our song* in the midst; our consciences *are affrighted*, lest we should speak a *falsehood* unto God; thus the powers of our souls are *shocked* on a sudden, and our spirits *ruffled—it almost always spoils* the devotion—our lips speak *nothing but the heart of David*. Thus our hearts are, as it were, forbid the pursuit of the song, and then the harmony and the *worship grow dull of necessity*. Many ministers and private Christians have long *groaned* under this inconvenience; there are a *thousand lines* in it—the Book of Psalms—which were not made for a church in our days to assume as its own. I should rejoice to see *David converted into a Christian:* there are *many hundred verses* in that book (of Psalms) which a Christian cannot properly assume in singing—as Ps. lxviii. 13, 16, and lxxxiv. 3, 6; Ps. lxix. 28, and Ps. cix. *are so full of cursings*, that they hardly become the tongue of a follower of the blessed Jesus. By that time they are *fitted* for Christian Psalmody—the composure can hardly be called *inspired or divine—*I could never persuade myself that the best way to raise a devout frame in plain Christians, was to bring *a king* or *captain* into our churches, and let him lead and *dictate* the worship in *his own* style of royalty, or in the *language of a field of battle.*"*

* Preface to Imitation, Works, Vol. 7, p. 24.

Another, Dr. James Latta, uses such language as the following: "Whether these psalms (*mentioned* 1 Cor. xiv. 26) were the effect of previous study and inspiration united, or of immediate suggestion, they were *certainly not designed* to inspire them—(the converts to the gospel) *with veneration and respect* for the Psalms of David. Any person will quickly perceive how *remote* psalms and hymns, formed upon it (the orthodox Nicene Creed) would be from the *doctrine* of the Old Testament. Nor do I think the introduction of the Psalms of David into the Christian church was very honourable to the cause of Christ. It deprived Him of divine honour—it deprived the asserters of His deity of *all* opportunity of bearing testimony to it in that part of their worship—it decided *clearly* in favour of that tenet of Arianism, that divine worship was to be paid only to the Father, and so had a *direct tendency to make heresy triumphant!*"*

The Psalms of the Bible—unchristian in spirit, in doctrine, unfit for devotion—tend to make heretics, &c.! How different this estimate of the inspired Psalter, from the testimonies to its excellence which we have furnished so abundantly in our first chapter! And in whose service, but in that of the infidel, were Dr. Watts and Dr. Latta employed in putting forth such utterances against the word of God?

Others have gone nearly as far, in other forms, in this work of undermining the faith of the church. They have virtually denied that the church—we speak in reference to her ordinary members—has, in her possession, the word of God at all: asserting, substantially, that there is no Bible, except in the original Greek and Hebrew. Mr. Black, against whose views on Psalmody Dr. Anderson composed his able work, thus wrote some sixty or seventy years ago: "'That there neither is nor can be any such thing as the *inspired*

---

* Discourse on Psalmody, 43, 51, 77.

forms of the psalms in our language, unless an immediate revelation were made in that language: that it is not possible to retain the words and phrases of the original in any translation; that as a prophet is to speak in the language which is suggested to him, his words are justly called the words of the Holy Ghost; but that whenever a translation of that subject is made into any other language, the words of the language into which it is translated are no more the words of the Holy Ghost, than Greek is English." We need not pause here to vindicate the claim of our Bibles as they are in the hands of the people of God, to be, indeed, the word of the living God. This is part of our controversy as Protestants with the Popish apostacy.

Another late writer follows in the same strain: "The inspired songs of the Old Testament are written in Hebrew, and that has been a dead language to her ever since her (the Christian church's) first existence. She might translate these songs: but the songs themselves she could not use."* And, of course, provided this be true of the psalms, it must be equally so of any portion of the Bible; and so, in his zeal against the exclusive use of the Scripture Psalms, this writer would take away from the plain people of God, the entire word of God: for, if the translated psalms are not the psalms, then the translated sermon on the mount, is not the sermon on the mount: if translated psalms occupy, substantially, the same position as the ordinary compositions of men, which express Scripture truth, then are the translated epistles of Paul to be regarded in the same light as other sound Gospel teaching; as to the *inspired* Paul's epistles, however, we cannot have them in our hands unless we can read Greek! These doctrines would deprive us of the Bible altogether: they would bereave the Church of Christ of any authoritative standard of faith and duty, accessible to *unlettered* Christians, and would hand these over

* Morton on Psalmody, p. 86.

to the teachings and interpretations of the learned, and especially to the clergy. Thus the Papists teach, reason, and conclude.

But this is not all. While at one time the claims of the Scriptures in the vulgar tongue are brought *down* to the level of ordinary compositions; at other times, the writings of men are exalted so as to bring them up to the height, at least, of the translated word of God. " And if the subject matter is inspired, that is enough; the song is an inspired song. For everybody knows, and the Doctor admits it, that the composition has its character from the subject matter. Every song, then, having for its subject matter inspired truth, is in reality an inspired song."* If this be so, then, every sermon which faithfully presents Gospel truth, every acceptable prayer as well as every sound hymn, must be " inspired" also! And then, so far from having no English Bible, as at other times seems to be taught, we have any number of them—they are beyond computation!

Another, of higher name, teaches, indirectly, the same singular doctrine. He says, " Human composure, properly speaking, is something, whether in prose or verse, composed by men, the subject-matter of which is human views, wishes, concerns, or interests. It is not proper to call a poem, the ground and substance of which is some doctrine, precept, promise, &c., in the word of God, a ' human composure.'" Dr. Pressly, among other judicious comments upon this remarkable definition of the phrase "human composures," says, " The reader will perceive that the author of the ' Inquiry' does not choose to appear before the public as the advocate of the use of songs of ' human composure,' in the worship of God. And to extricate himself from this difficulty, he has invented a convenient definition of the phrase, ' human composure.' He maintains that a composition, which has been written and arranged by man, provided the matter of it be taken from the

---

* Morton on Psalmody, page 92.

Bible, is not a 'human composure,' but is 'divine.' And according to this definition, every evangelical sermon in the world is a 'divine' composition! and Dr. Ralston's ' Brief Explication of the Principal Prophecies of Daniel and John,' is a 'divine' book! Against such an abuse of language, for the purpose of elevating the compositions of men to a level with the word of God, I enter my solemn protest."* And well he may: for it is more than an " abuse of language"—it is false teaching, calculated to mar the faith of the church.

It is not our purpose to enter into any detailed refutation of these heretical assertions and doctrines. Every champion of the church's common faith, as against infidels, Papists, and enthusiasts of all sorts, who pretend to share in inspiration, is equally bound with us to engage in this work. These are errors which assail the very foundations. We hold them up as beacons to admonish the reader to beware of entering upon that course of reasoning which has led to such conclusions as these, regarding the character and spirit of the Bible itself, and as to the fact whether we have any Bible at all, in any other tongue than the Hebrew and Greek, or even any Bible whatever, inspired in a way far transcending all that ordinary, even good teaching can claim.

Nor do we design to affirm, or even insinuate, that all who favour the singing of hymns, have gone these lengths. An Alexander, or a Junkin, would revolt at teachings like these, as sincerely as we do. But to these results, not a few, as we have seen, have been driven in their advocacy of hymn-making and hymn-singing in the worship of God. Nor can we exempt from all blame, the denominations in behalf of whose practice in this matter of psalmody these statements have been made: for we have yet to learn that these

---

* Pressly, p. 22.

assertions and reasonings have been met by any such rebuke on their part, as they certainly deserve.

It is no hallowed cause in which men, not deficient in sagacity, have felt themselves constrained, somehow, by an inexorable logic, to defend their views at such an expense. If hymns cannot be vindicated without disparaging the translated word of God and its claim to hold, when faithfully rendered, an incomparably higher place than the compositions even of the most enlightened and experienced Christians, their defence ought, by all means, to be abandoned.

VII. The introduction and the use of hymns, has been followed by the abandonment, to a very great extent, of congregational singing; and, even in domestic worship, there is, if we are not greatly mistaken, comparatively little use of sacred song. Hymns and "Imitations" of the Psalms have been, in a vast number of instances, the precursors of various appliances and arrangements in connexion with the musical services of the sanctuary; while these, again, have had the effect of closing the lips of the worshippers. So that, except in social meetings, we may safely assert, that in most denominations,* which favour the singing of uninspired songs, they often do not after all sing them, either in public or domestic worship! The great mass of the worshippers (?) in public service "sit mute"—to use an expression employed by a late writer respecting the Independent Churches of England—while a few in the choir attend to this part of the services. Is not this, notoriously, the fact? too notorious to require any proof! And, not in this land alone, but in others, r'though not everywhere to the same extent, the use of hymns has largely sent the entire "service of song" into some corner of the church edifice, committing it to a few, and these not always specially devout and solemn. In many congregations, the voice of a wor-

---

* The Methodist denominations do still, we believe, retain congregational singing.

shipper anywhere out of the choir-gallery, would be frowned upon as an unwarrantable interference with the artistic efforts of the select few! As to the devotions of the family, in this country at least, we are quite safe in asserting that they are generally conducted in hymn-singing denominations by reading the scriptures and praying alone; singing praise is omitted. Dr. J. W. Alexander says, "This part of the service (family singing) has fallen out of the practice of many households, and (strangely enough) extensively in those regions where scientific music has been most boastfully cultivated." "It is a remarkable fact, that in those circles of the religious world which consider themselves the most accomplished, there are many families where sacred music receives no separate attention . . .; when the hour of family worship arrives, *no hymn of praise ascends to God* . . .; our Christian daughters, practising for hours a day under great masters of singing, are sometimes unwilling to lend their aid even in the house of God." . . "We believe that the *revival* of psalmody in the house, would contribute to train voices for the sanctuary." "It is mournful to think, that a service which was so precious to our ancestors, and which they made sacrifices to enjoy, even when under the sword of persecution, *should die out in many Christian families* in these days of peace, when there is no lack of worldly rejoicings, ' and the harp, and the viol, tabret, and pipe, and wine, are in their feasts.'" (Is. v. 12.*)

There are exceptions: but the fact is indisputable, that congregational singing, and singing in family worship, have largely disappeared : † and a most singular fact it is. Claiming the right to sing anything they please—advocating a wide liberty of selection—boasting

---

* Dr. J. W. Alexander's Thoughts on Family Worship, pp. 218, 224, 226, 230.

† Some efforts are making to revive congregational singing; but with only partial success.

that they have found hymns—multitudes of them—more suitable for New Testament service of sacred song ; they do probably—*really sing nothing* at all—in the public—it may be in the domestic worship of God! Having banished the " psalms, hymns, and spiritual songs" which God has provided, adopting in their stead, either " imitations" of them, or hymns, they have gone on to a practical disregard of the ordinance of praise itself! They neither sing the Psalms of the Bible, nor any other!

Not so the psalm-singing churches. They retain congregational singing. In a very few instances, the choir principle *may* be adopted partially, but no where, we believe, can there be found a congregation which remits the exercise of praise to a few occupants of a gallery. And so of family worship. In psalm-singing denominations, both in this country and in Europe, the celebration of God's praise in the songs of Zion, is one part of the exercises of family worship. On this we quote from Dr. Alexander : " The use of psalmody in family worship we believe to have been almost universal (he might have said universal) in the Old Presbyterian Church of Scotland, as *it has been laudably kept up till this day*. That it tended, in a high degree, to increase the interest of all concerned in the service, and to promote Christian knowledge and sound piety, we cannot for a moment doubt."* All this has now mainly departed from *one* class of churches, while it has remained in another. Is there not a very solemn lesson, both of instruction and admonition, to be learned from this ?

But why has singing praise been dropped so extensively in connexion with the use of hymns ? We suggest the following : (1.) The hymns lack *authority*. It is very difficult to make out the call of God in the case of *any given hymn* at a given time. Even admitting that it is a duty to sing praise, the question rises as to the call to this duty in the given case. *We* have no

---

* Thoughts, &c., p. 222.

doubt at all that this radical defect in the entire system of hymns, has wrought gradually, but effectively, to produce the state of things we now witness, and so many deplore. (2.) And, in part, arising from the same cause, the idea of worship has ceased to no inconsiderable extent to be attached to the singing of hymns. We here use the words, and support our statement by the authority of the writer from whom we have already quoted: "Is the true character of this service that of worship? Probably few or none would, in form, deny it. Our hymn-books, however, and the usage of many Christian ministers and people *do deny* it, *in fact*. At least they hold it as a mixed service, partly worship and partly not. They sing now to God, and now to creatures. They do this, not only in mere musical exercises and recreations when there is no profession of worship, but also when households encompass the domestic altar, and the great congregation waits before God. As a Divine ordinance, then, the service of song is one of worship. This is the view of the Bible, the doctrine of the church, the usage of heaven. Like prayer, it is worship in its most direct form. What then? This. Thou shalt worship the Lord thy God, and Him only shalt thou serve. No creature, man or angel, may share this honour. It belongs exclusively to God. The conclusion is inevitable and urgent. It reaches our hymn-books. *It demands a material change in their character.* They are not formed on this definite and prime principle. Sometimes, indeed, they agree with it, as often they violate it. Whatever their compilers thought sufficiently pious and lyrical seems to have been inserted without a controlling reference to its fitness for the *specific purpose of worship.* They abound, therefore, with meditations, invitations, exhortations, expostulations, soliloquies, and even dialogues. Here they sing to creatures, and there to God; thus practically teaching that the one is as right and becoming as the other."*

* S. D., in the Presbyterian, Nov. 27th, and Dec. 4th, 1858.

(3.) The abandonment so largely of congregational singing, may be traced to that fondness for fine, scientific music, which has ever followed in the train of hymns, when used among a cultivated people. The associations of every day musical training and recreations, are readily transferred to the Sabbath, and the sanctuary. It is all the singing of songs : men's songs. These may differ in their subject, but they are one in their origin. Hence, unlike those who use the word of God alone in singing His praise, there is no particular sense of incongruity in treating hymns as other songs are treated—that is, made the mere vehicle of music, instead of employing music to deepen the impression of the sentiments uttered.

Whether we have traced the causes of this state of things accurately or not, our facts remain. They deserve high consideration.

VIII. The use of hymns in religious exercises endangers the church's purity : hymns may be used, and have been, in diffusing errors and heresy. That the songs used by the church in her devotions have no feeble influence upon her faith, we have already affirmed. The fact is beyond question. The notion of sacredness becomes, in some cases, attached to them. Their constant use impresses them deeply upon the mind, and upon the heart. Hence, error incorporated in songs and sung in devotional exercises, occupies the most favourable position possible. Corrupters of the faith have ever understood this well ; and, hence, have availed themselves of the instrumentality of songs as a most effective means of propagating their erroneous opinions. The Biblical Repertory, speaking of Bardesanes, says, "The Gnostic doctrines were poetic, and they were made popular, and widely extended by the *hymns* and *odes* of this heretical poet, and those of his more distinguished son, Harmonius."* Neander makes a similar

* 1829, p. 530.

statement regarding later generations: "and as sectaries and heretical parties *often had recourse to church Psalmody to spread their own religious opinions,* all those songs which had not been for a *long time* in use in the church, were particularly liable to suspicion."* And finally, the Repertory, alluding to the partisan use which the various factions of the church made of song, says, " Thus one of the most sacred portions of the worship of the church militant, in which it was designed to approximate most closely to the services of the church above, degenerated into the mere watch-word of a party, and the signal for strife and controversy."

We can trace, not very distinctly, but with sufficient clearness for the purpose of admonition and warning, the hurtful workings of this agency even in the hands of those esteemed orthodox. The author of the " Voice of the Christian Life in Song," thus speaks of the " Anonymous Greek Hymns"—" If any difference is apparent between the theology of these early hymns and that of St. Paul and St. Peter, it seems to be this: the incarnation and nativity of our Lord seem in the hymns to fix the attention, rather than His death and resurrection. The language would perhaps be rather— 'I was determined to know nothing among you, save Jesus Christ, and Him incarnate,' than, 'I was determined to know nothing among you, save Jesus Christ, and Him crucified.' And in some measure the results of this difference may be traced. There is great rejoicing in Christ as the Restorer and Saviour, great adoration of Him as God manifest in the flesh, but perhaps less apprehensive of Him as the Redeemer of sinners, the Lamb of God, who has washed us from our sins in His own blood; and, therefore, less apprehension of the completeness of the redemption, and the blessed security of the believer, living or dead. From this tendency to make the manger, rather than the cross, the centre of the faith, *probably arose those first mis-*

* His. ii. 318.

apprehensions of the position of the Virgin Mary, which afterwards spread so sadly." A perusal of these "Hymns" shows clearly enough that this is no unfounded surmise. The same author, sets up a token of warning when speaking of the one hymn of Clement.† " Through all the images here so quaintly interwoven, like a stained window, of which the eye loses the design in the complication of colours, we may surely trace, as in quaint old letters on a scroll winding through all the mosaic of tints, 'Christ in all.' And could the earliest Christian hymn bear a nobler inscription? Yet, at the same time, we must remember, that whilst the truth of the early Christian writings bears precious testimony to the Christian life of the times, *their defects and mistakes* bear, by contrast, no less valuable testimony to the inspiration of those earlier writings in which neither defect nor mistake is found." ‡

Ephraem Syrus was the great " orthodox" hymn-writer of the fourth century. But who was Ephraem? A monk of Mesopotamia—perhaps a pious man, but a believer in relics, in prayers to and for the dead, and in a kind of purgatory. The writer from whom we have just quoted, thus speaks of him : " His learning might seem foolishness to children among us, and his theology may fall far short of the fulness and simplicity of the Apostles' teaching; but his heart seems to have been steeped in the Gospel histories ; and, however dim might have been his explanation of the way of salvation in those Gospels, he surely found the Saviour, whom not having seen, he loved, and in whom he rejoiced with joy unspeakable and full of glory, receiving the end of his faith, even the salvation of his soul."§

It may be said, however, that his hymns may have been orthodox—that his errors found no place in them —and, hence, that Ephraem neither diffused nor confirmed errors by his songs. We admit that his hymns

---

* Voice, &c., pp. 27, 28. † Clement lived at the close of the second century. ‡ Voice, &c., pp. 45, 46. § Ibid, pp. 54, 55.

contain·much truth, and often beautifully and touchingly expressed. But they also contain more or less of his errors. The same writer, who admires him greatly, says again—" There is also a song of Ephraem's about Paradise, the feet of whose mountains the highest waves of the deluge could but touch and kiss, and reverently turn aside ; where the sons of light tread the sea like Peter, and sail the ether on their chariots of cloud. And there is a hymn on the resurrection, full of beautiful images, or rather visions ; the gates of paradise opening of themselves to the just ; the *guardian angel* striking his harp as he goes forth to meet them, when ' the Bridegroom comes with songs of joy from the East, and the kingdom of death is made desolate, as the children of Adam rise from the dust, and soar to meet their Lord.' There is mention also of a *fire to be passed through ere paradise is reached* (a fire not purgatorial, but testing), the unjust being devoured by it, and the just gliding through untouched."* We have here, with some idle fancies, an allusion to a " fire" after death, that might soon, to say the least, become " purgatorial." Finally, we present as we find it in the pages of Dr. M'Master, a stanza, from this author, recommending prayer for the dead.

>"Behold our brother is departed
>From this abode of woe:
>Let us pray in his departure
>That his guide may be propitious.
>Beatify him in the mansions above.
>May his eyes behold thy grace.
>Feed him with thy lambs."+

These fanciful notions and erroneous views, thus incorporated with the hymns of so popular a writer, could not fail to work injury. True, the age of Ephraem was one already quite distinctly marked by the adoption of many of the errors which developed rapidly

* Voice, &c., pp. 53, 54. + M'Master, p. 49.

J

into the Papal apostacy. It is also true, that this monk was among the most orthodox men of his day and place—he belonged to the East; but all the worse, when even he introduced into his hymns errors of such a character. His general orthodoxy, and the acknowledged excellence of many of his compositions, would give countenance, currency, and stability, to the false, the fanciful, and the visionary. Poison is all the more dangerous when mixed with wholesome viands.

When we come nearer to our own times—the middle ages, and since—we find the same agency used to establish errors. In the former, the monks sang, and others sang with them, of the "Virgin," and of the literal "cross," &c. "Long before error had been stereotyped into a creed, it has echoed from the hearts of the people *in hymns*. We need only study the sacred poetry of the middle ages to understand why the Reformation was needed. One painfully expressive fact meets us at the outset. Of Mone's 'Collection of the Latin Hymns of the Middle Ages,' in three volumes, one is filled with hymns to God and the angels; one with hymns to the blessed Virgin Mary; and one with hymns to the saints."* In our own day, what mean these confused sounds from the many denominational hymn-books? Why such hymn-books at all? The truth is, each embalms its peculiar views in song, and so endeavours to give them currency and permanence. Hence, nearly every fresh schism of any magnitude in these bodies, gives rise to some modifications in the "service of song."

That there is danger attending the use of uninspired songs in our days, *we* infer from the actual character of a large number of the hymns now in use. And this we prefer to give in the language of a writer upon whom we have already made a draught:—" The Plymouth compiler, in his 264th hymn, offers to 'Christian congregations,' as a help to worship, this song to Mary:

* Voice, &c., p. 200.

'Why is thy face so lit with smiles,
  Mother of Jesus! Why?
And wherefore is thy beaming look
  So fixed upon the sky,' &c.

"Suppose we turn to the 'Lyra Catholica,' and from the same composition add another verse:

'Why do not thy sweet hands detain
  His feet upon their way?
O, why doth not the mother speak,
  And bid her son to stay?'

"What! In our social and public worship sing to the Virgin Mary? That were downright Popery. Shades of Luther, Calvin, Knox! has it come to this? Were your great labours in vain? Take care, thou excited Protestant! People who live in glass houses must not throw stones. You do in the service of song, in the house of the Lord, just as the Papists do. Protestants and Papists alike sing to creatures. The only difference between them, in this matter, is not one of principle, but of taste. And here they have the advantage of us. They have a higher standard. They sing to the angels, to the Apostles, to Mary, and the noble army of martyrs and confessors. We, on the contrary, excluding these, except now and then the angels, sing to all sorts of inferior creatures, and especially to sinners. These last have a large place in our hymnology. They are, indeed, highly honoured. We may sing to them in our worship at pleasure, though they would crucify the Saviour afresh. But what a prodigious stir would there be in our churches, should we venture to sing such stanzas as *the above, to Mary!* For our part, we condemn both."*

It may be said, that the most objectionable hymns are excluded from the devotions of the more evangelical churches. That may be; but none the less are they in the hands of many professing Christians, and in general circulation: claiming a *status* among the sacred

* S. D., in the Presbyterian, Dec. 11th, 1858.

songs of the age, and doing their part towards moulding its views.

If we would occupy safe ground, let us keep to the "psalms and hymns and spiritual songs" of the Word of God. These are pure—in them is no error. *They will never contribute anything to the already sufficiently extended influences that tend to mislead the minds and corrupt the hearts of sinful men.*

In some of these arguments we may find reasons ample to vindicate the divine wisdom and goodness in linking the "service of song" in the house of God, with an inspired manual. To give license here to human ingenuity, hazards the interests of truth and purity; tends to confirm disunion; fosters a worldly taste and undue fondness for mere vocal or instrumental melody; inflicts upon the church the evil of an insatiate desire of novelty and change: and may even put an end, as it has already done so extensively, to the joint and hearty co-operation of "all the people" in the exercise and ordinance of praise.

CHAPTER IV.

THE SUITABLENESS OF THE PSALMS FOR NEW TESTAMENT WORSHIP, AND THEIR USE VINDICATED AGAINST OBJECTIONS.

The necessity for such a vindication of the inspired psalms, is certainly to be regretted. The very fact of their inspiration, should be, of itself, an answer to nearly every objection, and their acknowledged excellence (see Chapter I.) should be ample for the refutation of others. Our task here is rather an ungracious one, but must be undertaken, inasmuch as those who use hymns, not satisfied with claiming a license to make and employ uninspired compositions in divine worship, have used no little ingenuity in the discovery of objections to the employment of the Psalms of the Bible in celebrating the praises of God in our devotions. Some of these objections may bear more directly upon their exclusive use—some of them may be urged by those who after all admit the *propriety* of their use with some exceptions and modifications; some of them, as we shall see, go much farther, and assail the psalms themselves.

I. It is said that the psalms speak of a Saviour to come, and, hence, are not suitable, nor designed to be used since His advent. We might satisfy ourselves here with the reply, that the use of the psalms, by almost universal acknowledgment, "passed over to the New Testament Church:" in other words, that they were used in the apostolic church, and, of course, with apostolic sanction. This has already been amply shown: and also, that in the best and purest times, the psalms have been held in the highest estimation as the matter of the church's praise in song: and that in every age they have been read and studied with singular satisfaction and edification by the most eminent saints of God. By considerations such as these, we would confute this objection; so far, at least, as it embraces a conclusion adverse to the use of the psalms under this dispensation. We prefer, however, to meet the objection—premises and all—directly, in the words of Dr. Pressly:—" It is taken for granted, in the objection, that if in the psalms, the church praises God for a Redeemer to come, therefore they are not suitable for the church now, since He has come. But it so happens, that every where in the psalms, the Redeemer of the church is presented to the view of our faith, not as one who should appear in some distant age, but as already engaged in the accomplishment of his Mediatorial work. In the 22d Psalm, the Redeemer is exhibited before our eyes, as suffering in the garden and on the cross; and we hear him uttering the very words which dropped from his lips while suspended upon the cross—'My God, my God, why hast thou forsaken me?' Again, He is presented to our view, as having triumphed over death and the grave, and having ascended on high; angels, principalities, and powers, being made subject to Him. And the church praises Him, not as a promised Saviour, but as an ascendant and triumphant Redeemer:—'Thou hast acended on high, thou hast led captivity captive: thou hast received gifts for men; yea, for the rebellious also, that the Lord God might dwell among them.' (Ps. lxviii. 18.) Permit me now to call the attention of the objector to a difficulty in which his principle involves him. If it were true that the psalms speak of a Saviour to come, and therefore are not suited to gospel worship, then those numerous psalms which speak of a suffering, risen, and ascended Saviour, were not suited to the worship of the Old Testament church, because the Redeemer had not then appeared in human nature. That is, though these psalms were given to the church by the God of infinite wisdom, to be employed in His worship, they were not adapted to the end for which they were given! O vain man! who art thou that repliest against God?

"But is it true, that the psalms present the Saviour to the view of our faith, as one who was yet to come? Is it really so, my venerable Father, permit me respectfully to ask—is it the truth that in the psalms given to the church under the Old Testament, she praised God for a promised Redeemer, who had not yet come? It is true that these psalms were composed long before the actual appearance of Jesus Christ in human nature. But it is no less true that these divine songs are the productions of that omniscient Spirit, before whose view all futurity is spread out, and things which were then future, are described by him as now taking place, or already past. For example, in the 22d Psalm, we hear our suffering Redeemer exclaiming, 'I am poured out like water, and all my bones are out of joint; my heart is like wax; it is melted in the midst of my bowels. The assembly of the wicked have enclosed me; they pierced my hands and my feet.' Again: This same glorious personage is presented to our view, as exalted upon the holy hill of Zion, in the character of God's anointed King, and proclaiming defiance to the opposers of His kingdom: 'Why do the heathen rage, and the people imagine a vain thing?' Again, He is described as coming to judgment, and all nature is summoned to pay obeisance to Him—'Let the heavens rejoice, and let the earth be glad before the Lord, for he cometh to judge the earth; he shall judge the world with righteousness, and the people with his truth.' If the principle assumed in the objection were well founded, that psalms which exhibit a promised Saviour, who is yet to come, are not suited to gospel worship, it would then follow that a large portion of the psalms are better adapted to the worship of the church now than they were formerly; for in them, the Redeemer is described as already come, a man of sorrows and acquainted with grief; as having risen from the dead; as having ascended on high, and as having received gifts for men. But the truth is, there is no force in the objection at all. Ever since the first promise of a Saviour was given to our lost world, Jesus Christ has been the only hope of sinful man. By faith in Him, as exhibited to them upon the infallible testimony of God, believers were saved under the Old Testament; and it is by faith in Him, as revealed to us upon the testimony of God in the gospel, that believers now are saved. The merit of the Saviour's death was as effectual in securing the salvation of the believer, before He actually laid down His life a ransom for many, as it is now. And those divine songs, in which His Spirit taught the church to praise Him, before the period of His incarnation, are, in all respects, as well adapted to the edification of the church now, as they were in the beginning. Not only so—I do not hesitate to say, that they are now better adapted to this end, as, in consequence of the light which the gospel has reflected upon them, the fulness of their meaning may be more thoroughly understood."*

II. It is that the psalms are encumbered and obscured by Old Testament allusions and phraseology. Is this so? Most assuredly it is not. The entire statement is untenable. We take for granted that the objection is not intended to bear against the record which the psalms contain of God's gracious providence towards His church of old. The historical psalms are as suitable now as ever for the service of praise. The facts recorded, and the power, energy, faithfulness, and wisdom of God, as the Redeemer and King of His church, which these facts illustrate and magnify, are as appropriate topics of praise in the heart and upon the lips of the New Testament worshipper, as ever they were.

As to sacrifices and offerings, these are rarely alluded to in the psalms, and in some of these instances they are only alluded to in the way of asserting their inefficacy. Omitting such phrases as "sacrifices of joyfulness," of "thankfulness," of "righteousness," which can give rise to no difficulty whatever, we find but five psalms—other than historical—in which any reference is made to this part of the ceremonial service —nine, or rather seven allusions in all—some of them being mere repetitions in the same verse. Of these, three or four are introduced accompanied by the assertion of their absolute inefficacy. As to the remainder, we direct the reader to the following remarks, from the pen of Dr. Pressly—"What, I would ask, was the meaning of the true worshipper under the law, when he came before God with such language as that employed in this psalm (the 66th)? Did he depend upon the sacrifices of fatlings, of bullocks, and of goats, for

---

* Dr. Pressly on Psalmody, pp. 93—96.

acceptance with God? Most certainly he did not. Through the medium of these bloody sacrifices, he, in the exercise of faith, looked to the Lamb of God, who taketh away the sins of the world. He depended, for acceptance with God, upon the same great sacrifice for sin, which is now the foundation of the Christian's hope. If then, the ancient believer could approach unto God acceptably in the use of such a song—if, while he had before the eye of his body a bleeding lamb, he had presented to the eye of his faith the Lamb of God—if the language of such a song raised in his breast pious affections, and aided devotion, why should such expressions and such language 'sink our devotion and hurt our worship,' since we have the light of the gospel to render their import more intelligible? If these and similar expressions did not 'bedarken the thoughts' of the ancient believer, and hide the Saviour from his sight, why should they have on us so injurious an effect? If such language served to lead the ancient Israelite to Him who is the desire of all nations, why may it not now raise the thoughts of the humble Christian, surrounded as he is with clearer light, to Him who is the end of the law for righteousness to every one that believeth?"*

Mention is made, occasionally, of musical instruments used in the Jewish temple service. Similar language is used, moreover, in the Book of Revelation, which speaks (chap. v. 8, xx. 2) of the redeemed as having "harps in their hands." Of course this language cannot be taken literally: it must be figurative, and shows clearly that the allusions to instruments of music in the psalms may be appropriated by the worshipper now in the same sense in which we explain these of the visions of the Revelation, as expressive of the liveliness which should ever characterize the spiritual emotions and services of the saints of God.

* Pressly, 105, 106.

If countries, nations, mountains, &c., are mentioned, as they occasionally are in the psalms, either these are but specimens, or they are used synecdochically, a part for the whole; or to invest the song with life and spirit, upon a well-known principle, recognized by all the schools of rhetoric—particular objects put for general and abstract statements—while many of these objects, moreover, were typical of spiritual things.

The truth is, no objection could be more groundless than this one. The psalms are singularly characterized by their adaptation to all times and lands. They are manifestly designed for all times and lands. They anticipate a time when all lands shall join in the worship of God, Creator, Redeemer, King. They have in them very little of the temple. The New Testament itself is almost as open to this objection as the psalms. Mr. Sommerville thus pertinently discusses the matter in this aspect—"The use of terms borrowed from the ancient economy is authorized by the example of New Testament writers. They describe the character, duties, the worship, and the privileges of Christians in the language of the people of Israel. The consistency of the language of the psalms with the spirit and the institutions of the present time will appear from the subsequent parallelism, suggested by a comparison of the terms employed by the penmen of the psalms with those introduced in the New Testament, unless it should be said that there is something 'Jewish and cloudy' in the writings of Christ and His Apostles, which is removed by the more lucid modes of speech which some of their more spiritual followers may teach us to use:—

PSALMS.	NEW TESTAMENT.
Ps. xlvi. 4. There is a river, the streams of which shall make glad *the city of God*, the holy place of the tabernacles of the Most High. xlviii. 2. Beautiful for situation, the joy	Heb. xii. 22. But ye are come unto *mount Zion*, and unto the *city of the living* God, the heavenly *Jerusalem*. Rom. ix. 6, 7, 8. They are not all *Israel* which are of Israel:

of the whole earth, is Mount Zion, on the sides of the north, the *city* of the great *king*. li. 18. Do good in thy good pleasure unto Zion: build thou the walls of *Jerusalem*. liii. 6. Oh that the salvation of *Israel* were come out of *Zion!* When God bringeth back the captivity of his *people*, Jacob shall rejoice, and *Israel* shall be glad.

Ps. xxvii. 4. One thing have I desired of the Lord, that will I seek after; that I may dwell in the *house of the Lord* all the days of my life, to behold the beauty of the Lord, and to inquire in his *Temple*. xlviii. 9. We have thought of thy lovingkindness, O God, in the midst of thy *Temple*. lii. 8. But I am like a green *olive tree* in *the house of God*.

Ps. liv. 3. For *strangers* are risen up against me, and oppressors seek after my soul. cxxxvii. 4. How shall we sing the Lord's song in a *strange land!*

Ps. cvi. 4, 5. Remember me, O Lord, with the favour that thou bearest unto *thy people:* O visit me with thy salvation: that I may see the good of *thy chosen*, that I may rejoice in the gladness of *thy nation*, that I may glory with thine *inheritance*. cxxxii. 9. Let thy *priests* be clothed with righteousness. cxlviii. 14. He also exalteth the horn of *his people*, the praise of all his *saints;* even of the children of Israel, *a people near unto him*.

neither, because they are the *seed of Abraham*, are they all children: but, in Isaac shall thy seed be called. That is, they which are the children of the flesh, these are not the *children of God:* but the *children of the promise* are counted for the *seed*. Gal. vi. 16. Peace be on them, and upon the *Israel of God*.

Jno. ii. 19. Jesus answered and said unto them, Destroy this *temple*, and in three days I will raise it up. 1 Cor. iii. 16. Know ye not that ye are the *temple* of God, and the Spirit of God dwelleth in you? 1 Tim. iii. 15. That thou mayest know how thou oughtest to behave thyself in the *house of God*, which is the *church* of the living God.

Eph. ii. 19. Now, therefore, ye are no more *strangers* and *foreigners*, but *fellow-citizens* with the saints, and of the *household* of God.

1 Peter ii. 9. But ye are a *chosen* generation, a royal *priesthood*, a *holy nation*, a *peculiar people;* that ye should show forth the praises of him who hath called you. Col. i. 12. Giving thanks unto the Father, which hath made us meet to be partakers of the *inheritance* of the saints in light.

Ps. xlii. 4. When I remember these things, I pour out my soul in me: for I had gone with the *multitude*, I went with them to the house of God, with the voice of joy and praise, with a multitude that kept holyday. cxxii. 3, 4. *Jerusalem* is builded as a *city* that is compact together: whither the *tribes go up*, the *tribes of the Lord* unto *the testimony of Israel*, to give thanks unto the name of the Lord. For there are set *thrones of judgment*, the *thrones of the house of David*.

Eph. i. 10. That in the dispensation of the fulness of times, he might *gather together in one all things* in Christ, both which are in heaven, and which are on earth; even in him. Heb. xii. Ye are come unto the heavenly Jerusalem, and to an *innumerable company of angels*, to the *general assembly* and *church* of the first born, which are written in heaven, to God the judge of all, and to the spirits of just men made perfect, and to *Jesus* the Mediator of the New Covenant. Luke i. 32. The Lord God shall give unto him (Jesus) the *throne of his father David*.

Ps. l. 5. Gather my saints together unto me; those that have made a covenant with me *by sacrifice*. lxvi. 15. I will offer unto thee burnt *sacrifices* of fatlings, with the incense of rams; I will offer bullocks with goats. cxviii. 27. Bind the *sacrifice* with cords, even unto the horns of the *altar*. xliii. 4. Then will I go to the *altar* of God, unto God my exceeding joy.

Rom. xii. 1. I beseech you, brethren, by the mercies of God, that ye present your bodies a living *sacrifice*, holy, acceptable unto God. 1 Pet. ii. 5. Ye also, as living stones, are built up a spiritual house, an holy *priesthood*, to offer up *spiritual sacrifices*, acceptable to *God by Jesus Christ*. Heb. xiii. 10. We have an *altar* whereof they have no right to eat who serve the tabernacle.

Ps. cxxxvii. 1, 8. By the rivers of *Babylon*, there we sat down, yea, we wept when we remembered Zion. O daughter of Babylon, who art *to be destroyed; happy shall* HE *be that rewardeth thee, as thou hast served us.*

Rev. xvii. 5. And upon her forehead was a name written. Mystery, *Babylon*, the great, the mother of harlots, and abominations of the earth. xviii. 20. *Rejoice over her*, thou heaven, and ye holy Apostles and Prophets; for *God* hath avenged you on her.

"Before a comparison of the mode of expression used in the psalms with that which is found in the

New Testament, every objection to the use of the songs of Zion, on account of the frequent allusions which they contain to the nature and circumstances of the religious institutions of Israel, vanishes. It is not intended to make the impression that there is no allusion to the types in the Book of Psalms, which is not found introduced by Christ and His Apostles to describe spiritual things. But we find them using figurative language derived from all the *leading* and *primary* characters of the former economy; and in this they furnish an evidence of the correctness and consistency of *Christians*, putting the name of the type to express the *thing typified*."* Finally, even Dr. Watts himself—who seems to have originated this objection, and certainly has stated it most strongly—has the following :—

> "Before thine *altar*, Lord,
> My *harp* and song shall sound
> The glories of thy word."

III. It is said that the psalms are not adapted to a season of religious reviving. This objection could scarcely be offered by one acquainted with the psalms themselves, and with their history. We have already asserted and shown that the psalms do give expression to the liveliest Christian emotions and affections—that they have been singularly esteemed and loved; habitually read, and studied, and sung, by many of the most spiritually-minded and devoted of the servants and ministers of Christ. Surely, the Apostolic church was a living and active church, but it is acknowledged that the psalms were then sung; and so far as the evidence goes, no other religious songs. The Waldenses sang the psalms and nothing else in their Alpine valleys; and in their seasons of persecution found in these inspired psalms, strength and hope. The French church,

---

* Sommerville, pp. 24—27.

and the churches of Switzerland, used nothing else in song, during the palmiest days of their religious life; while these sacred songs contributed no little to the spread of the gospel.* These psalms constituted the only psalmody of the Scottish church in her first and second Reformations. These were the songs whose melody was heard in the cottages, in the glens, in the moors, and on the mountains, and often on the scaffold and at the stake, in the dark days of Scottish persecution. In these psalms, the multitudes who waited upon the preaching of Livingston, celebrated God's praises in that day of the Lord's power when five hundred souls were converted by means of one sermon at the Kirk of Shotts. The thousands who turned to the Lord, flocking as "doves to their windows" during the season of genuine and extensive reviving subsequent to that day, used none but Bible Psalms. These psalms were the sacred songs of the revived church in Ireland, in the days of the Bruces, the Welshes, the Blairs, the Cunninghams, and Livingstons, when large districts were aroused and turned, almost as one man, to God.† The early Presbyterians of this country, used none

---

* The following is taken from Lorimer's "Protestant Church in France," p. 19, Phila. ed.—"In 1535, the Scriptures were translated into the French language, by Olivetan, the uncle of the celebrated Calvin, and shortly after the Psalms of David were turned into verse by one of the popular poets of the day, and set to melodious music. This last undertaking was attended with remarkable success. There had been nothing of this kind before, and so the whole music of the people was perverted to sinful and superstitious purposes. Now, the national genius was enlisted on the side of truth. 'This holy ordinance,' says Quick, 'charmed the ears, heart, and affections of court and city, town and country.' This one ordinance alone, contributed mightily to the downfall of Popery and the propagation of the gospel. . . . No gentleman professing the Reformed religion would sit down at his table without praising God by singing. Yea, it was an especial part of their morning and evening worship to sing God's praises."

† Reid's History of the Presbyterian Church in Ireland.

other, during those "golden days, when souls were enlightened with such a knowledge of Christ, as if the light of the sun had been seven fold, as if the light of seven days had poured at once on the worshipper with healing in every beam."*

The Bible Psalms *are* adapted to any season of *genuine* reviving of religion. They have been tried. They have never been found wanting. The revival to which these psalms are not adapted, should itself be suspected.

IV. It is said that the psalms are difficult to understand; and, perhaps, it may be insinuated that this is virtually acknowledged by some who use them, inasmuch as they formally explain them in their public exercises. This is an objection which we would not be surprised to find in the mouth of a Papist, who, on this alleged ground, refuses the Bible to the common people, and refers them to what he styles the plainer and safer teaching of a priest; but we would hardly have looked for it from any one, who, as a Protestant, holds that the Bible is not an unintelligible book. We admit, indeed, that the psalms, in common with other Scriptures, are characterized by an inexhaustible fulness of meaning; but we deny that they are, in any peculiar degree, hard to understand. The truth is, they are much more intelligible than many other portions of the Bible. They present fewer difficult passages—scarcely any in fact; and, in the main, are singularly clear. They have ever been favourite *reading:* the pious have enjoyed them with a special relish. *They* have found none of this asserted obscurity in these sacred songs, but rather an unusual, and, generally, transparent clearness, while the less studious, or thoughtful, or spiritual, alone complain that they are obscure. We quote with satisfaction the following judgment of the distinguished Dr. Horsley: "Of all

* Webster's History, p. 124.

the books of the Old Testament, the Book of Psalms is the most universally read; but, I fear, as little as any understood. This cannot be ascribed to any extraordinary obscurity of these sacred songs; for of all the prophetic parts of the Scriptures they are certainly the most perspicuous. But it is owing, partly, I fear, to some *dulness* of the faculties of the natural man upon *spiritual subjects.* There is not a page of this Book of Psalms in which the *pious reader will not find his Saviour, if he reads with a view of finding Him;* and it was but a just encomium of it that came from the pen of one of the early Fathers, that it is a complete system of divinity for the use and edification of the common people of the Christian church."* Scott the distinguished commentator says, " There is nothing in true religion, doctrinal, experimental and practical, but will present itself to our attention while we meditate upon the psalms. And hardly an occasion of praise and thanksgiving can be conceived, to which some portion of them, *faithfully* rendered in poetical versions, may not be applied with peculiar energy and propriety; and indeed the Christian's use of them in the closet, and the minister's in the pulpit, will generally increase with the *growing experience of the power of true religion in their own hearts.*"† A correspondent of the " Presbyterian Magazine," bears like testimony—" The very *excellence* of the Book of Psalms has, in this, its effect. Their depth of matter, their spirituality, their sublimity, their transcendent elevation of devotion, raise them above the comprehension, and above the standard of devotional feeling of ordinary Christians. It is a fact, that Christians of deficient attainments often find themselves more edified in reading other books than the Bible, and really relish them more. But the higher Christians rise in gracious experience, the higher is their esteem for the pure word of God, until at length,

---

* Quoted by M'Master, p. 131. † Preface to Psalms.

every human production becomes insipid in comparison therewith. As it certainly can have no good effect to promote in the public mind, a preference of other books, to the Bible, so it is conceived there can no good effects arise from promoting in the public taste a preference of other compositions to the psalms the Holy Spirit hath inspired."*

As to the exposition of the psalms, if this is an acknowledgment of such obscurity in the psalms as is impenetrable to ordinary intellect, why not apply the same principle to other Scriptures? to the Sermon on the mount? to the Ten Commandments? to the Lord's Prayer? These are explained, and re-explained, in every pulpit; but who imagines that he is confessing, while engaged in such an exercise, that the Bible is unintelligible? These expositions are all " helps :" they aid the reader, the inquiring, the Christian. And so with the " Explaining of the Psalms :" it is designed as a help to the better understanding of the psalms, and to quicken the mind and heart, as the worshipper is about to enter upon the exercise of praise. Yet, even this is entered upon but rarely, compared with the whole number of times the psalms are sung. Finally, if there be in the psalms a depth of meaning— if there be some parts of them requiring investigation, this is a reason for the careful study of them—a reason for endeavouring to bring up the Christian intelligence to a higher level, and not a reason for degrading the exercise of praise to the level of the heedless and uninquiring capacity.

V. It is said that the Book of Psalms is unsuitable for the use of children. If so now, it must have been fully as much so, at the least, when God gave it to His church. Besides, whatever force there may be in this objection, the psalms share with the rest of the word of God. Part of both *are* intelligible, not to infants, but to children of some development and education;

* Presbyterian Magazine, July 1822, quoted by M'Master.

and as they grow in ability and wisdom, and, of course, more capable of understanding the Scriptures, they become better acquainted also with the psalms. The children of the Jews, of the Apostolic church, of the French, Swiss, and Holland Reformed, of our Scottish forefathers—were not comparatively deficient in Christian knowledge: nor are the children of the psalm, singing churches now. None of them have lost anything by the want of little religious songs. Instead, their minds were and are strengthened by early familiarity with songs so superior in acknowledged excellence.

We go further. We deny that the psalms are uninteresting to the young. Many of them—as thousands can testify—are highly attractive, and become, from an early age, imprinted upon the hearts of the children of the church. This is all that we can fairly ask. It were a singular principle to apply to the worship of God, that every thing in it must be adapted throughout, or even mainly, to the easy comprehension of the very young. Must we have a "child's Bible as well?"

VI. It is said that the psalms are not adapted to the condition and experience of every worshipper. If this be an objection, it must have been, as some we have already noticed, an equally solid reason why the psalms *never* should have been sung in the worship of the church, either in Old or New Testament times. The objection is, moreover, equally good against any hymn-book whatever: for the special circumstances, the experiences, &c., of all the worshippers, will scarcely ever be identical in any worshipping assembly. And finally, this objection leaves out of view the fact, that in singing psalms, God is praised. And, hence, the joyful Christian may praise Him for deliverances wrought for the sad and afflicted: the sad and afflicted may praise Him for the promises and tokens of His favour which fill the heart of the emancipated believer with joy and gladness. Both can celebrate His works of power and of mercy in behalf of His church and kingdom, while both may see in the tones of grief and sorrow, and again in the notes of exultation and triumph, the heart of a Saviour once suffering, now exalted.

VII. It is said that churches which use hymns are more prosperous—grow more rapidly—than those that do not. It might be enough to reply, that mere statistics settle no principle of moral or religious truth. Rome reasons in this very way. Few Christian communities have grown as rapidly as the Mormons or the Spiritualists. But does the objection state the fact? It may be that, in some localities and times, the assertion of the objector may be true. But it is not true when we regard the matter as we should, in a more comprehensive spirit. When has there been a more rapid increase in numbers than in the Apostolic age? or in the era of the Reformation? If psalm-singing churches do no not grow so rapidly now, it must be owing, not to their psalmody, but to other causes.

Again, mere growth in numbers is no criterion of a church's real prosperity. Growth is, indeed, eminently desirable. It is a ground of rejoicing, high and holy, when multitudes flock to Zion; but we must look beyond this: we must have regard to other elements of true and lasting prosperity. If mere additions to the numerical strength constitute any argument in behalf of doctrines and practices, then Presbyterianism is less worthy of acceptance than Methodism, for the latter has grown the most rapidly—Methodism less worthy of acceptance than the Baptist views and system, for the latter grows most rapidly of all. Does the Most High endorse *all* these varying doctrines by blessing with increase those who hold them? And is His approbation, in the degree of it, to be measured by this increase? The fact is, the Most High may and does bless His own truth, even when it is presented intermingled with some error; to ascertain what is truth, we have but one resort —"the law and the testimony."

Still, we do not admit that the growth of the psalm-singing churches *is* even in this day so much less than the growth of others as the objection requires. We believe they will bear scrutiny well on this point. Most of them, so far as we can judge of statistics, are not far behind any of their contemporaries. And should there even be some ground for the objection, may it not be owing rather to the fact that the use of the psalms has generally been found associated with a closer adherence to Scriptural requirements in the admission of members, and a more careful discipline exercised over those within?

VIII. It is said that the spirit of some of the psalms is inconsistent with that of the New Testament—in fact, that some of them are unchristian.

This objection is thus stated by Dr. Watts—" I have been long convinced, that one great occasion of this evil arises from the *matter and words* to which we confine all our songs.* Some of them are *almost opposite to the spirit of the Gospel;* many of them foreign to the state of the New Testament, and widely different from the present circumstances of Christians. Hence, it comes to pass, that when spiritual affections are excited within us, and our souls are raised a little above this earth, in the beginning of a psalm, we are checked on a sudden in our ascent toward heaven, by some expressions that are most suitable to the days of *carnal ordinances*, and fit only to be sung in the *worldly sanctuary*. While we are kindling into divine love, by the meditations of the loving kindness of God, and the multitude of His tender mercies, within a few verses, some *dreadful curse against men* is proposed to our lips, which is so contrary to the new commandment of loving our enemies."

To this we reply—(1.) That assertions of this kind would be altogether consistent—coming from those who deny the inspiration of the scriptures; or rather, from those who go farther, and condemn the Bible as a bad

---

* In 1712, Songs of Presbyterian Churches "confined" to the psalms.

book; but we cannot understand how such an objection can be offered, or thought of, by any one who believes that the psalms are a part of the inspired word of God. It does appear to us very like the language of blasphemy, if it be not the language of infidelity. (2.) It is a fact sufficiently remarkable, that those very psalms which are styled pre-eminently "cursing psalms"—the 69th and the 109th—are among the number of those psalms which we can on the most unquestionable testimony identify as directly appropriated to the betrayer of our incarnate and suffering Saviour. They are both quoted, and in the most striking manner, in the New Testament—Acts i. 20—and are spoken of as "scripture, which the Holy Ghost by the mouth of David, spake before concerning Judas." (3.) *Our Saviour himself used these very psalms*: they are His language. In proof of this we have but to examine the psalms themselves, taking with us the above inspired interpretation of them. It will be seen that the *speaker* is no other than Jesus himself. It is He that speaks of the traitor in the terms of fearful but just denunciation, which Dr. Watts, and many since his day, have ventured to denominate unchristian?*

(4.) Finding these and similar utterances in the psalms, it would be wisdom in the objector, to study carefully their import, and then, seek to have his mind and heart brought into conformity with the Spirit of Christ speaking in them—a spirit of eternal justice and holiness.

(5.) If we must do so, however, let us inquire, whether the Spirit of Christ in David did really move him to utter unchristian sentiments? Here we quote from Sommerville: "If the psalms have been dictated by the Holy Ghost—if by the Spirit of Christ, who speaks not of himself, but speaks what he hears, the character of the author determines the character of the Book.

* Let the reader turn to these psalms and satisfy himself in this respect.

If God, the author, be holy, there is nothing unholy in the Book of Psalms, or calculated to encourage unholiness; if God be merciful, there is nothing in it inconsistent with mercy, or calculated to encourage cruelty; if God be love, there is nothing in it contrary to the spirit of love, or calculated to encourage hatred or revenge; in one word, there cannot be anything in the book opposed to any perfection of the Divine character, or failing to recommend conformity to God upon the part of man. Whoever, therefore, quarrels with the spirit or matter of the psalms, sets himself in opposition, not to man, but God, for he implicitly imputes to God whatever he charges upon his word.

"Or again. The inspiration of the psalms and of the New Testament being taken for granted, if the psalms do not manifest the same spirit, inculcate the same doctrines, enjoin the same moral duties, prohibit the same sins, which are set forth in the New Testament, it follows that the Holy Ghost is inconsistent with himself. But it would be no difficult matter to show that the spirit, the doctrines, the precepts, the prohibitions—in a word, the design and tendency of both are the same. And we know that the Old Testament saints—we know that David possessed and exemplified that very character which the Gospel of Christ recommends. Will any man venture, upon mature consideration, to set declarations from the pen of David, especially remembering that it was guided by the Spirit of God, the expression of whose inflexible justice, of whose detestation of sin, of whose determination to punish it—to all which holy men of God have been enabled—to which David was enabled to say, Amen—he may have mistaken for the language of unforgiving cruelty; will any man venture to set declarations, the spirit and design of which may be misunderstood, in opposition to facts? Are malignity and revenge rashly to be imputed to the man, who found his enemy in a cave—his enemy who had attempted his life, who was at that moment in pursuit of him, attended by three thousand men, that he might overtake and kill him—and would not put forth his hand against his person, though urged by his followers? Will we attribute malignity and revenge to him who, coming into the camp of his adversary by night, and finding him and his men asleep, neither injured him nor would permit another to do it, though solicited, and could show the sword and cruise of water which he .had carried away from his head, a testimony at once of his own power to have taken revenge, and of the simplicity an l ingenuousness of his temper and conduct? Was the man malignant and revengeful, who, when an ungrateful rebel in the day of adversity cursed him and vilified his character, could say, profoundly resigned to the award of Heaven, 'Let him alone, and let him curse ; for the Lord hath bidden him.' And shall we join with the many who have conspired to vilify the character and the words of the sweet singer of Israel, even at the hazard of charging the Spirit of Christ with want of consistency? God forbid. . . . Once more, and I dismiss this branch of the inquiry : Is such language as this cruel? 'Cut them off in thy truth.' 'I will bring again from the depth of the sea ; that thy foot may be dipped in the blood of enemies, the tongue of thy dogs in the same.' 'Let them be blotted out of the book of the living, and not be written with the righteous.' Is it inconsistent with the spirit of the Gospel, to use it with the character of the Christian? Mark the consequences. Then the words of Paul, moved by the Holy Ghost, not merely writing to the church, but to a bishop of the church, must share in the same condemnation. 'Alexander the coppersmith did me much evil : the Lord reward him according to his works.' (2 Tim. iv. 14.) If the spirit manifested in such portions of the psalms as those quoted be unchristian, by what spirit shall we say the Apostle was actuated? If the psalms be inconsistent with the Gospel, then Paul must be inconsistent with himself, for in the sixteenth verse we read, 'At my first answer no man stood with me, but all forsook me: I pray God that it may not be laid to their charge.' Let him who is straitened in the use of some portions of Zion's songs, explain the consistency of the fourteenth and sixteenth verses of the fourth chapter of the second epistle to Timothy, and he shall find himself near an enlargement. Another consequence follows. The saints enter into the regions of love and peace, with all the cruelty and revenge of earth about them. 'And when he had opened the fifth seal, I saw under the altar the souls of them that were slain for the word of God, and for the testimony which they held: and they cried with a loud voice, saying, How long, O Lord, holy and true, dost thou not judge and avenge our blood on them that dwell on the earth?' Finally, God must delight in carnage, and be chargeable with encouraging cruelty in His people. The great God has a supper, to which the fowls of heaven are invited, that they may 'eat the flesh of kings, and the flesh of captains, and the flesh of mighty men, and the flesh of horses, and of them that sit on them, and the flesh of all, free and bond, both small and great.' 'I heard,' says John, 'another voice from heaven, saying, Come out of her, my people.' This must be the voice of God himself, for who else claims the saints for his own? And what does the voice proclaim in addition to a call to come forth from among the children of mystical Babylon? Reward her even as she has rewarded you, and double unto her double according to her works: in the cup which she hath filled fill to her double. Rejoice over her, thou heaven, and ye holy apostles and prophets; for God hath avenged you on her." (Rev. vi. 10; xviii. 4—6; xix. 17, 18.*)

(6.) Finally, we affirm, that it is one of the true and

---

* Sommerville, pp. 48—49.

godlike excellencies of these psalms—whatever sentimentalists may say—that they do celebrate the awful justice of God, the most righteous Lawgiver and Judge, " to whom belongeth vengeance"—His justice in vindicating His truth, His people, and the claims of His Son, and in visiting as they deserve, the malignant and impenitent enemies of the Person, the throne, the grace, of Jesus Christ. Let us hear Tholuck—" In modern times the opinion seems to obtain, that love to enemies is enjoined as a duty in the New Testament only. The gratuitousness of that opinion is apparent from consulting correct translations of Lev. xix. 18; Ex. xxiii. 4, 5; Prov. xxiv. 17, 18, 29; xxv. 21, 22; Job xxxi. 29. To form a right estimate of the misgivings alluded to, we should consider the *end contemplated by punishment*. The common view is, that, with God and the pious, punishment springs from *love*, and contemplates the improvement of man. But what is to be done if you have to deal with an incorrigible sinner? The *end* of improvement, therefore, cannot exhaust the purpose of punishment. Philosophy agrees with Christianity, that the specific purpose of punishment is *retribution*, *i.e.*, the welfare of the individual is to be disturbed in the same measure as he has disturbed or infringed upon the law of God or the state. Hence it appears, that to deny the punishment of a hardened sinner (not on personal ground, but from a sense of the holiness of the divine law) is as little to be regarded as evidencing moral imperfection, as it would be to desire that those who are susceptible of improvement should, by means of correctives, be brought to their senses. The objection is met, if it can be shown that the imprecations and prayers for Divine punishment do not flow from the vindictive disposition (viz., personal irritability and passion) of the Psalmists, but from the motives just now alluded to. Those supplications would then correspond to the earnest desire of a good monarch, or a just judge, to discover the guilty, that justice might be administered; and the expressions of David, the private individual, ought to be referred to those noble motives which developed the principles he uttered when a king. (Ps. ci. 8.)

"The Psalmists frequently state sentiments like the following, as the motives of their prayers for the punishment of their enemies—that the holiness of God and his righteous government of the world should be acknowledged, that the faith of the pious should be strengthened, that they should praise God, that the haughtiness of the ungodly should be brought within bounds, that they should know that God is the righteous judge of the world, and that the fulfilment of His glorious promises should not fail."*

IX. It is said, that if we sing the psalms we must also sing the titles to the psalms: and as some of these titles allow the use of instruments, that we must also use them. It is added, that in the Hebrew Bible, the title is often marked as the first verse. To this we remark: (1.) That, at best, this can be no argument against using the psalms. If the titles were really meant to be sung, or if the psalms were designed to be always sung in connexion with the instruments referred to, this much would be gained by the objector, *but no more*. (2.) Does any one believe that the title "Psalm of David," &c., was ever meant to be sung? or ever was sung? or that no Jew was allowed to sing these psalms in the ordinary services of religion without using the "harp," &c.? (3.) As to the division of psalms into verses—as these are marked in our Bibles—this is a modern affair altogether. (4.) The authenticity of these titles is not universally acknowledged. Let this point be settled first. (5.) We follow, in omitting the titles, the example of our prose version, which never marks the title as being part of the psalms. (6.) When the objector can tell us precisely what these instruments

* Tholuck on Psalms, p. 42, 43.

were, it will be time enough to inquire about their claims. In fact, they belonged to the temple, and were not used in the ordinary worship even of the Jews.

In fine, we repeat: as to many of these objections, there is a spirit in them so adverse to a Scriptural faith, and a true piety, that the very fact that they are adduced on behalf of the use of hymns, constitutes a distinct, and by no means feeble, argument against them. A cause which resorts to such a course of reasoning is not a good one. We should fear and eschew it.

CHAPTER V.

SOME REMARKS UPON THE SCOTTISH VERSION OF THE PSALMS.

WE have thus far kept before us but one definite proposition—the Psalms of Scripture faithfully rendered, the church's sufficient and appointed manual of praise, to the exclusion of all uninspired hymns and songs. We have sought to establish and vindicate this proposition, irrespective of every question regarding the merits of a particular version. And here we might leave the entire subject; for we are persuaded that, if our proposition were generally admitted, there would be little controversy in reference to the particular version in which the psalms should be sung: all would be resolved into the single inquiry—important at the same time—as to the claims of any version, or professed version, to be a true and accurate rendering of the words and sentiments of the inspired Psalmist. This could be quite readily and amicably settled, as it has been settled in other ages, and in other lands, to the entire satisfaction of the church and the people of God.

It is well known, however, that the controversy on the subject of psalmody has, of later years, been largely complicated with that of the merits of the version usually styled "the Scottish version." Of this version, the advocates of the use of hymns have—many of them—allowed themselves to speak in terms expressive of everything but respect. They speak of it rather scornfully, as "Rouse," or as "Rouse's Psalms." They criticise, with the utmost severity, its rythm and its grammar; while, with some exceptions, they do, notwithstanding, admit its fidelity to the original Hebrew. They seem, in a word (we refer still to the many, not to all) to view it as deserving only of the most contemptuous treatment, and assert that it holds its place in the esteem and love of the psalm-singing churches merely through the power of prejudices imbibed by early education and long usage. Hence, we feel ourselves warranted, if not obliged, to append, as we now propose to do, a few remarks upon this particular version. And,

1. It cannot, with a due regard to Scriptural truth, and a proper reverence for a faithful translation of the Word of God, be styled "Rouse," or "Rouse's Psalms," nor even, in absolute terms, "Rouse's version." True, indeed, this version is mainly due to the labours of an eminent scholar and gentleman of that name, a member of the Assembly of Divines, at Westminster, but was subjected to a careful scrutiny, first in England, in the year 1645.* They made amendments. It was then transmitted to Scotland, and again examined and revised with the utmost care. Aiton, in his Life of Alexander Henderson, refers to this version of the psalms as follows—"The version of the psalms by Roos (Rouse) was intended not only for the Church of Scotland, but also for that of England, during the general prevalence of Presbyterianism. After all pains in England had been bestowed upon the psalms, they were sent down to Scotland in portions for further consideration. The Church of

* Neil's History of the Puritans. vol. i. p. 388. London, 1837.

Scotland appointed John Adamson to revise the first forty psalms, Thomas Crawford the second forty, John Row the third, and John Nevey the last thirty Psalms. The committee were enjoined not only to observe what needed amendments, but also to set down their own method of correcting. It was recommended to them to make use of the travails (*i. e.*, labours) of Rowallin, Zachary Boyd, or any other on that subject, but especially of the then existing Paraphrase (version) so that whatever could be found better in any of these works might be adopted. The version thus purified by the Scottish committee was sent to all the Presbyteries of the church, who transmitted their observations to the original committee. These reported their labours on the remarks from the Presbyteries to the Commission of the Assembly for Public Affairs. After the Commission had revised the whole, they were sent to the Provincial Synods, and through them again transmitted to the Presbyteries: and after their further consideration, the version, thus fully prepared, was sent up to the General Assembly. The version so prepared was then "allowed by the authority of the General Assembly of the Kirk of Scotland, and appointed to be sung in congregations and families" (1649): and thus it was finally adopted, superseding, by its acknowledged merits, the versions previously in use both in Scotland and England. Hence, this translation is not absolutely "Rouse's." It has received the *imprimatur*, after amendment, of the most learned assembly, perhaps, ever convened on earth; and of another, the Scottish Assembly, not much inferior.

Now, we have an English Bible: a translation from the original Hebrew and Greek, made by forty-seven learned men of the English Universities, who divided themselves into six companies for the purpose.* They had been called together by King James I. Did we know, as we do not, the name of the particular individual

* Neal's History, vol. i. 454.

who prepared the first draught of the Book of Proverbs, what would be thought of the spirit of the professing Christian man, who would indulge, habitually, in speaking of the Book of Proverbs, not as the Proverbs of Solomon, but as " Bilson's Proverbs," or " Smith's Proverbs :"* or even as " Bilson's version," or " Smith's version ?" Would this be tolerated as decent, or becoming? We think not. How do a large part of the religious community now, regard the contemptuous flings sometimes made at our English Bible, as " King James' Bible ?" Luther translated the Bible into the German tongue: what would be thought of the man who would constantly speak with contempt of the German Bible, as if it were not God's Bible, but "Luther's ?" And yet none of these translations were subjected to such scrutiny of competent authority and learning, as this version, which grave men permit themselves scornfully to speak of in no other terms than " Rouse's Psalms," or, at best, " Rouse's version :" sometimes asking whether Dr. Watts had not as good a right to *make* Psalms as Rouse.

2. In view of the facts which we have just presented, we are, certainly, at liberty to pronounce, very decidedly, the " Scottish version" to be an accurate rendering of the original. We are aware, indeed, that attempts have been made to disparage it even in this respect, but they have signally failed. In fact, it is even less liable to the charge of inaccuracy than our generally faultless English Bible. Where it differs from the prose, competent judges pronounce most frequently in its favour as really the more accurate. Hence,

3. Between this version and Dr. Watts' " Imitations," for example, there can be no comparison on the score of fidelity. Dr. Watts did not profess to render the psalms into English verse : his design was, and so declared, to *make* psalms, taking the Scripture as a kind

---

* To these men the publishing of the translation was committed. We use their names for illustration merely.

of basis. Hence, *he* never called his work a " version;" he says " he *imitated*" the Psalms of David, " in the language of the New Testament." How he has performed his work, Dr. Cooper has thus shown: " He (Dr. Watts) expressly says, in his preface, 'It must be acknowledged that there are a thousand lines in it (the Psalms of David) which were not made for the church in our days to assume as its own.' Of course they have been omitted. Where, then, is the imitation of these thousand lines? He further tells us that he 'has entirely omitted several whole psalms, and large pieces of many others;' where is the imitation of these psalms? But has he left them out as unfit to be used in the worship of God? No; had he merely done this, our feelings would have been far less shocked. He has given the whole one hundred and fifty 'Psalms of David, in metre,' though several whole psalms, and large pieces of many others have been entirely omitted, according to his express declaration. Let us look, for instance, at the 109th psalm. The original, as we have it in our prose and in our metrical translation, contains thirty-six verses; that of Dr. Watts contains six verses, and there is not an idea in the one to be found in the other, unless it be the address in the first line, ' God of my praise.' The psalm, as it comes from God, is taken up with a fearful description of the awful doom of his implacable enemies, and is applied in the New Testament to Judas. The subject of Dr. Watts' imitation—of Dr. Watts' '*version*,' is ' Love to enemies from the example of Christ.' Can there possibly be a greater perversion of language than to call this a version of the 109th psalm? and yet they charge the friends of an inspired psalmody with excluding Dr. Watts' ' rich and beautiful version of the psalms from the sanctuary.' What would he think if the Apocryphal psalm, in the Septuagint version of the psalms of David, were published to the world, and used in the worship of God as one of the Psalms of David, and shall he think it 'strange' that we are unwilling to admit into the sanctuary, as a version of the Psalms of David, psalms which, in the language of the pious Romaine, 'are so far from the mind of the Spirit, that I am sure if David were to read them, he would not know any one of them to be his?' How could we regard with feelings of complacency their introduction into the sanctuary, as a version, believing, as we do, with Professor Alexander of Princeton, that they are '*all* intended to be used in public worship;' and believing, also, with the same author, that 'the arrangement of the psalms was the work of Ezra, the inspired collector and *redacteur* of the canon.' No, we cannot so regard their introduction. We must continue to protest against it, however strange our opposition may appear to the admirers of what they call 'Dr. Watts' rich and beautiful version of the psalms.'"*

4. We do not, however, claim perfection for the Scottish version of the Psalms. We are well aware that its rhymes are frequently defective, that it contains some obsolete words, and that its rhythm is sometimes at fault. This is only saying, what all acknowledge respecting our English Bible—that it is susceptible of amendment. But like that Bible, the work of amendment will need to be gone about very cautiously, lest the fidelity of the words and the vigour of the style be impaired in the process.

But is this version so rude as is often asserted? Is it justly, and necessarily offensive to a cultivated Christian taste? We say, without hesitation, it is not. We have ample evidence that it is not; for it has commended itself to not a few of the best minds for its evident faithfulness, its fulness, its nervous energy, and even for its highly lyric character of style. Nor do we go back to the days of the Westminster Assembly for our proofs. We find them in the fact, that this version is

* What Drs. Breckenridge and Junkin think of Watts' "Imitations" we have already seen.

now used, or has been, even in these late days, with satisfaction by men whom the world knows well as singularly accomplished—such men, for example, as are now, or others who lately were, the ornaments of the Scottish and Irish Presbyterian Churches: to say nothing of many in the psalm-singing churches in this country. We have other testimonies. The eminently accomplished and pious author of the "Life of Faith" —Romaine—thus replied to some who thought it strange that he should use the version of Sternhold and Hopkins—"They wonder I would make use of this version, which they think is poor, flat stuff, the poetry is miserable, and the language low and base. To which I answer, they had a scrupulous regard for the very words of Scripture, and to these they adhered closely and strictly; so much as to render the versification not equal to Mr. Pope. I grant it is not always smooth; it is only here and there brilliant. But what is a thousand times more valuable, it is generally the sentiment of the Holy Spirit. That is very rarely lost. And this should silence every objection—*it is the word of God*. Moreover, the version comes nearer to the original than any I have ever seen, *except the Scotch*, of which I have made use, when it appeared to me better expressed than the English. You may find fault with the manner of ekeing out a verse for the sake of the rhyme, but what of that? Here is everything great and noble, although not in Dr. Watts' way or style. It is not like his fine sound and florid verse: as good old Mr. Hall used to call it, *Watts' jingle* I do not match those psalms with what is now admired in poetry: although time was when no less a man than the Rev. T. Bradbury, in his sober judgment, thought so meanly of Watts' hymns as commonly to term them *Watts' whymns*. And, indeed, compared to the Scripture, they are like a little taper to the sun; as for his psalms, these are so far from the mind of the Spirit, that I am sure if David was to read them, he would not know any one of them to be his."* M'Cheyne (himself a poet) says—" The metrical version of the psalms should be read or sung through, at least, once a year. It is truly an admirable translation from the Hebrew, and is frequently more correct than the prose version." Even Sir Walter Scott (no mean authority in matters of taste and poetry) says—" The expression of the old metrical translation, though homely, is plain, forcible, and intelligible, and very often possesses a rude sort of majesty, which perhaps would be ill exchanged for mere elegance. I have an old-fashioned taste in sacred as well as profane poetry: I cannot help preferring even Sternhold and Hopkins to Tate and Brady, and our own metrical version of the psalms to both. I hope, therefore, they will be touched with a lenient hand." Rufus Choate, of Boston, is at all events a man of taste. He has said—" An uncommon pith and guarled vigour of sentiment lies in that old version: *I prefer it to Watts.*"

It were well, indeed, could the fidelity of this version be combined with a more entire exemption from the minor faults which attach to it. But, in the meantime, we would, with myriads of the saints of God, prefer to have the Word of God as the matter of our praise, rather than the most flowing and smooth of mere human utterances.

* This same Romaine wanted words to describe what he thought of those who supposed they could make " better psalms than those of the Bible."

APPENDIX A.

Psalms for both Testaments.

IN addition to the more direct argument by which we have established in our 2d chapter, the permanent appointment of the Book of Psalms as the church's manual of praise, we quote the following from the pen of the learned author of "The Typology of the Scriptures;" embodying in our quotation the high commendations of this book from the pen of another distinguished writer:—

"These psalms are chiefly summaries, in a poetical and impressive form, of great truths and principles, derived from the past acts and revelations of God, by some of the most gifted members of the church, and accompanied with such pious reflections and devout breathings of soul, as the subjects naturally suggested, through God's Spirit, to their minds. In them is expressed, we may say, the very life and essence of the symbolical institutions and manifold transactions in Providence, through which the members of the old covenant were instructed in the knowledge, and trained to the service of the true God— and so expressed as to be most admirably fitted for forming the minds of all to right views and feelings concerning God, and enabling them to give due utterance to these in their exercises of devotion. But was this the character and design of the Book of Psalms merely to the Old Testament Church? Is it not equally adapted for the suitable expression of pious feeling, for a help to devotion, for a directory of spiritual thought and holy living, to the church of the New Testament? Is there a feature in the Divine character as now developed in the Gospel, a spiritual principle or desire in the mind of an enlightened Christian, a becoming exercise of affection, or a matter of vital experience in the Divine life, of which the record is not to be found in this invaluable portion of holy writ? And how could such a book have existed among the sacred writings centuries before the Christian era, but for the fact that the old and new covenants, however much they may have differed in outward form, and however the transactions respectively connected with them may have been inferior in the one case to the other, yet were alike pervaded by the same great truths and principles? Thus the Book of Psalms, standing mid-way between both covenants, and serving equally to the members of each as the handmaid of a living piety, is a witness of the essential identity of their primary and fundamental ideas. *There* the disciples of Moses and of Christ meet as on common ground, the one taking up as their most natural and fitting expressions of faith and hope, the hallowed words, which the other had been wont to use in their devotions ages before, and then bequeathed as a legacy to succeeding generations of believers. So intimately connected were they with the affairs and circumstances of the dispensation, which was to vanish away, that they one and all took their occasion from these, and are fraught throughout with references to them; and yet, so accordant are they to the better things of the dispensation that abideth, so perfectly adapted to the ways of God as exhibited in the Gospel, and the spiritual life required of its professors, that they are invariably the most used and relished by those, who are most established in the grace, and most replenished with the blessing of God. It was confessedly carnal institutions, under which the holy men worshipped, who were employed by God to indite these divine songs, as it was also the transactions of an earthly and temporal life, which formed the immediate ground and occasion of the sentiments they unfold; yet where in all Scripture will the believer, who 'worships in spirit and in truth,' more readily go to find language for expressing his loftiest conceptions of God, for portraying his most spiritual and enlarged views of the character he is called to maintain, or breathing forth his most elevated desires and feelings after divine things? So that the psalms may well be termed, with Augustine, 'an epitome of the whole Scriptures,' and a summary, not as Luther said, of the Old Testament merely, but of both Testaments together, in their grand elements of truth and outlines of history. 'What is there necessary for man to know,' says Hooker, 'which the psalms are not able to teach? They are to beginners an easy and familiar introduction, a mighty augmentation of all virtue and knowledge in such as are entered before, a strong confirmation to the most perfect among others. Heroical magnanimity, exquisite justice, grave moderation, exact wisdom, repentance unfeigned, unwearied patience, the mysteries of God, the sufferings of Christ, the terrors of wrath, the comforts of grace, the works of Providence over this world, and the promised joys of that world which is to come, all good necessarily to be either known, or had, or done, this one celestial fountain yieldeth.' We may, therefore, conclusively appeal to the character of this extraordinary book, as confirmatory of the general views, which it has been our object to establish. It renders clear as noon-day the perfect identity of those great truths and principles, on which both economies were founded as to the institutions of worship, and the providential dealings respectively connected with them. And as we know the one to have been all arranged in preparation for the other, consequenty in pre-ordained connexion with it, we thus learn what was the real nature of the resemblances, which formed the connecting link between the things of the two covenants, and, how we are to explain the one as types and the other as antitypes."

APPENDIX B.

The correspondent " S. D." of the Presbyterian—from whom we have taken some *facts* in regard to the hymns now in use, but without intending to endorse *all* his theories—denies that the psalms were *all* intended to be sung, even under the Old Testament dispensation; of course, while he finds fault with the hymnology of the age, he also denies the appointment of the Book of Psalms, as a whole, for the use of the church in New Testament times; quoting as his only authority—for he gives no argument—Dr. Davidson of England. We also can give authorities much superior in their character to that of a writer who was obliged to relinquish, on account of his Rationalistic views on the subject of Inspiration, the position which he had long held as Professor in the Lancashire Independent Theological Seminary.

Dr. J. W. Alexander, speaking of the psalms, says, " *all* intended to be used in public worship."

Tholuck, a comparatively orthodox German (Introduction, p. 2)—" The psalms have ever since the first

---

* Fairbairn's Typology, &c., pp. 60—63. Ed. 1852.

century, formed an *essential* part of Christian worship."

Herder, another of the same stamp, says of the Book of Psalms, "it is the hymn-book for all times."

Edwards, the most eminent theologian of the Western world, in a passage from which we have quoted already, but which we give here in full, is most express. He says :—

"Another thing God did towards this work, at that time, was his inspiring David to show forth Christ and His redemption, in divine songs, which should be for the use of the church, in public worship, *throughout all ages.* This was also a glorious advancement of the affair of redemption, as God hereby gave His church a book of divine songs for their use in that part of their public worship, viz., singing his praises throughout all ages to the end of the world. *It is manifest the Book of Psalms was given of God for this end.* It was used in the church of Israel by God's appointment: this is manifest by the title of many of the psalms, in which they are inscribed to the chief musician, *i.e.*, to the man that was appointed to be the leader of divine songs in the temple, in the public worship of Israel. So David is called *the sweet Psalmist of Israel*, because he penned psalms for the use of the church of Israel; and accordingly, we have an account that they were actually made use of in the church of Israel for that end, even ages after David was dead; as 2 Chron. xxix. 30—'Moreover, Hezekiah the king, and the princes, commanded the Levites to sing praises unto the Lord, with the words of David, and of Asaph the seer.' And we find that the same are appointed in the New Testament to be made use of in the Christian church in their worship. Eph. 5 19: 'Speaking to yourselves in psalms, hymns, and spiritual songs.' Col. iii. 16: 'Admonishing one another in psalms, hymns, and spiritual songs.' *So they have been and will, to the end of the world, be made use of in the church to celebrate the praises of God.* The people of God were wont sometimes to worship God by singing songs to his praise before, as they did at the Red Sea: and they had Moses' prophetical song, in the 32d chapter of Deuteronomy, committed to them for that end; and Deborah, Barak, and Hannah sung praises to God; but now first did God commit to his church *a book of divine songs for constant use.*"*

* Edward's Works, vol. iii. pp. 230—232. N.Y. Ed. 1820.

Hymn Writers.

We have barely touched in Chapter III. upon the character of the hymns now in use, nor do we propose to do so here. Many of these are very nice songs: some of them beautiful in sentiment and in style, some of them very touching and pathetic; but there are some facts in regard to the authorship of some of the hymns sung in evangelical churches that should be known. A hymn-book was compiled a few years since by Rev. H. W. Beecher, the (*) correspondent of the "Independent." In reference to this book, the Evangelist, he says:—

"Charged that in collecting hymns we have gone quite beyond the ordinary excursions of evangelical compilers of hymn-books, and have freely used 'Catholic, Unitarian, Universalist, Swedenborgian, and other collections.'"

The compiler thus vindicates himself and his collection:—

"Our reply is a denial that we have gone where *other evangelical compilers have not gone.* There is scarcely a collection made within thirty years, that has not been indebted to *Catholic, Unitarian,* and *Universalist* collections. The *Church psalmody* prepared by Lowell Mason, and Dr. Greene, one of the officers of the American Board of Foreign Missions; the *Psalmist,* the standard Baptist collection, edited by Baron Stow and S. F. Smith, and adopted by the Board of the Baptist Publication Society; and especially the Methodist Episcopal collection, approved by Bishops Hedding, Waugh, Morris, Hamlin, and Janes, published by the Methodist Book Concern, and now generally used by that denomination; the Lutheran collection, published by the General Synod of the Evangelical Lutheran Church—all these, and many others, *are indebted largely to Catholic, Unitarian,* and *Universalist* collections. As for the Swedenborgian collections, we cannot tell how much we may owe to them, as we have never seen one."

The author says again:—

"The Evangelist charges that in the Plymouth Collection there is a '*large admixture*' of the hymns of Bryant, Chapin, Furness, Willis, Mrs. Hemans, Tom Moore, L. E. L. (Letitia

Landon), Longfellow, Mrs. Sawyer, Whittier, Festus Bailey, Burns, Miss Martineau,* and others."

And thus answers :—

"What are the facts? We do not know of a single evangelical collection of hymns which has not introduced the hymns of *some or many of these authors.* In the book of the General Association of Connecticut, hymns of Bryant, Pierpont, Bowring, Hemans, Martineau's Collection, Pope, Sir Walter Scott, Tom Moore, are all found. In the New School Presbyterian Assembly's book, *Tom Moore holds an honourable place,* as he does in the book of the Old School General Assembly, and Nettleton's Village Hymns. When the General Assemblies join in giving to the church TOM MOORE's '*Come ye disconsolate, where'er ye languish,*'† we think the *Evangelist* need not take the pains to sacrifice its candour and veracity in order to reproach the Plymouth Collection for having Tom Moore's '*mock piety.*' In the Baptist Collection may be found Mrs. Follen, Bulfinch, hymns from Martineau's Collection, *Tom Moore,* Mrs. Hemans, Pope, and Willis. The Methodist Collection contains hymns of *Moore,* Bryant, Ware, G. P. Morris, Pierpont," &c.

The only vindication proposed is, "If the hymn is good, we are not to go behind it. . . . The hymn is to stand for itself." This may satisfy some, but we are much mistaken if the plain people of God are prepared to offer the Most High the effusions of all sorts of heretics. This is a painful feature of modern hymnology. The hymns of such writers may be good poetry and pretty reading, but to use them in God's worship is, we think, most offensive to Christian faith and feeling. How dare a worshipper come before God with thoughts and words which, it may be, an open enemy of Christ has furnished him? The Reformed Church of Germany, a section of the large Protestant body, seems to have come to this conclusion. At the Conference of the present year, held at Elberfield, it was decided that "*only hymns whose authors are known*

* An Atheist.
† A favourite hymn with many; a hymn, moreover, if we mistake not, with rather a remarkable history for a hymn. Moore was a Papist, and a very free and *luscious* poet.

to be *truly regenerate Christians shall be received."* Consistently carried out, this decision will exclude from this service all but the Bible Psalms ; for how is it to be determined, beyond possibility of mistake, that the authors of any others are "truly regenerated Christians?"

APPENDIX D.

In connexion with the argument of our third chapter, in regard to the use of hymns, an inquiry arises, whether songs, such as those which are often prepared and sung on anniversary occasions may be consistently sung? In this we remark—1. That were Christians agreed in reference to the subject in the aspect in which it has been before us — the use of hymns in worship — this inquiry would give little trouble. If such songs were used at all, it would be only as patriotic songs, for example, are sung on public occasions, or as songs are sung in private circles, for musical recreation or practice, and not under the name of devotion at all. 2. Whether they are so sung, generally, in the circumstances to which we allude, we cannot tell. We presume, however, that in many cases, the idea of worship does not present itself to those who use them. It certainly cannot, in instances of which we have seen notices, in which the children, and perhaps the adults, of a congregation unite in singing a song prepared as an expression of their welcome to a pastor, and in all such like instances. Still—3. Inasmuch as these are not necessary (as there is no obligation to use such songs, as the propriety of their use may be often, at least, doubtful), and inasmuch as these are associated in some degree, perhaps largely, in the public mind with the use of hymns in the worship of God, and may be regarded as such worship, we think it is not only wisest and safest, but required of us, to avoid them. We might add, that this whole thing is liable to what we regard as very gross abuse; for example, we have seen a statement of a pastor being sung *to* on the *Lord's day*, by an assembled Sabbath-school!

APPENDIX E.

The following summary answers to arguments for the use of hymns, and to objections to the use of the psalms in worship, are taken from a condensed summary on the subject of psalmody, annexed to Rev. R. J. Dodd's "Reply to Morton."

" It is objected—

1. 'That the singing of uninspired composition, in divine worship, is not forbidden in the word of God.'

Answer. Neither are we forbidden to observe seven sacraments. In determining whether or not this or that particular service should be made a part of God's worship, the absence of divine appointment, amounts, in all cases, to a prohibition.

2. 'That good men have composed hymns to be used in divine worship, and sing hymns of human composure.'

Answer.—1. The best of men are liable to do things which will dishonour God, and injure the church. 2. There are many good men who would not dare, either to compose a song to be sung in divine worship, or to offer to God a song composed by man.

3. 'That those who use human psalmody, are more numerous than those who use only the book of Psalms in singing God's praise.'

Answer.—1. It was not always so; and the time may yet come, when it will cease to be so. 2. The multitude *are not always*—nor have they hitherto *commonly been right*, in matters of faith, and religious practice.

4. 'That we are allowed to compose our own prayers, and, by parity of reason, ought to be allowed to compose our own songs of praise.'

Answer.—1. Right or wrong, it is a matter of fact, that most worshippers neither do nor can compose their own songs of praise. 2. God has given us, in the Bible, a Book of Psalms, but no book of Prayers; and promised to the church a Spirit of prayer, but not a Spirit of psalmody. 3. In prayer we express our own wants; in praise we declare God's glory. If we can frame a form of words, suitable for the former purpose, it by no means follows that we are equally competent to compose a form of words for the latter purpose. 4. The ordinances of prayer and praise differ in this—that in the former the thoughts suggest the words ; and we should therefore use the words which they do suggest; whereas, in the latter the words, are designed to suggest the thoughts, and therefore we should use words, if such we can obtain, which can suggest none but appropriate thoughts. 5. Our wants are always changing; and, therefore, our prayers should vary : but the glory of God is ever the same ; and therefore the same collection of songs will serve for the expression of His praise, from age to age.

5. 'That there is, in the New Testament, authority for singing songs composed by men.' *First:* we are referred to the fact that Christ and His disciples sung a hymn. Matt. xxvi. 50. *Answer.*—1. Let it be proved that the hymn sung by our Saviour and the disciples, was not one or more of the Psalms of David. It is supposed by the best commentators, to have been the *great hallel,* consisting of the Psalms from the 113th to the 118th inclusive. 2. Our Saviour was better qualified, and had a better right to compose hymns than Dr. Watts, John Wesley, Philip Doddridge, &c. *Second :* It is argued that Paul enjoins the use of uninspired psalmody when he says, Col. iii. 16, 'Let the word of Christ dwell in you richly in all wisdom ; teaching and admonishing one another, in psalms, and hymns, and spiritual songs ; singing with grace in your hearts to the Lord.' Some argue from the first clause of the verse, ' Let the word of Christ dwell in you richly in all wisdom;' explaining the phrase, 'the word of Christ,' to mean either the whole Bible, or the New Testament; and alleging that the Apostle enjoins the use of songs drawn from the whole word of God, or from the New Testament in particular. *Answer.*—1. Let it be proved that this expression means either the whole Bible, or the New Testament, and not simply, the principles of the gospel. 2. Let it be proved that the Apostle enjoins upon the church, to compose songs, drawing the matter of them from what he denominates ' the word of Christ.'

Others reason from the use of the three terms, 'psalms, and hymns, and spiritual songs' in the latter clause of the verse. *Answer.*—1. No good reason can be assigned, why any one of the psalms of inspiration might not, in reference to different aspects under which it may be viewed, be denominated a 'psalm, hymn, and spiritual song.' Such a use of language is not uncommon. God says Ex. xxxiv. 7, ' forgiving *iniquity,* and *transgression,* and *sin.*' 2. If these three terms designate three distinct kinds of devotional poetry, let it be proved that the Book of Psalms does not comprise songs of these three different kinds. 3. The Jews applied the terms psalms, hymns, and songs, indiscriminately to the Book of Psalms.—See Josephus, Philo, &c.; and the same may have been done by Paul and the primitive Christians. 4. In the Septuagint, which was the translation of the Old Testament in use in the days of Paul, some of the psalms are, in their titles, designated *psalmos*—a psalm; others, *ode*—a song; and others, *alleluia;* which last is a word borrowed from the Hebrew, and when used as a noun in the Greek language, is equivalent to *hymnos*—a hymn. Why may we not suppose the Apostle has allusion, in this verse, to these three terms used in the Septuagint version, as titles of different psalms?

Third: it is inferred from 1 Cor. xiv. 26, that the Corinthians brought to their assemblies psalms composed by themselves, under a supernatural impulse of the Spirit, and of course not contained in the Book of Psalms. *Answer.*—Let it be *proved* that the psalms, by the unseasonable utterance of which they disturbed their assemblies, were composed by themselves under an impulse of the Spirit, and not selected from the Book of Psalms.

6. 'That the Book of Psalms is hard to understand.'

Answer.—1. If there are some passages in the psalms hard to understand, so are there in the other scriptures.—2 Pet. iii. 16. 2. It is no harder to understand the psalms when we sing them than when we read them. 3. The more we use them, the better will we understand them. 4. *We* have a better opportunity of understanding them than Old Testament worshippers had; and we are sure the Book of Psalms was *their* psalmody. 5. If we are unable to understand the psalms, much less are we able to compose songs which will supply their place. 6. If any man does not understand the psalms, let him, under the direction of their divine Author, endeavour to ascertain their meaning. 7. The psalms are not, in general, hard to understand. There is, indeed, an unfathomable depth of meaning in them; but no man finds fault with a well on account of its depth, if the water rises to the surface. There can be more divine truth, and true devotional sentiment found on the very face of the inspired psalms, than can be obtained from those which are uninspired, when they are worn threadbare.

7 'That the psalms are not adapted to New Testament worship.'

Answer.—1. God never changes, and of course His praise is always the same. 2. The **Spirit of God** was better able, in the days of David, to prepare songs suited to New Testament worship, than *men* are now. 3. The psalms everywhere speak most clearly of Christ and His mediatorial work, kingdom and glory; and are, by the Apostles, copiously quoted in illustration of the way of salvation. 4. They make less reference to the peculiarities of the old dispensation, than some books of the New Testament do. 5. We have no Book of Psalms in the New Testament, and no command to prepare one.

8. 'That the psalms contain sentiments adverse to the spirit of the Gospel; abounding with sharp invectives against personal enemies, and being, in many instances, expressive of revenge, &c.'
Answer.—It is blasphemy.

9. 'That the psalms are not sufficiently copious to furnish a complete system of psalmody.'
Answer.—1. God is no more glorious now than He was in Old Testament times ; and if the psalms were sufficient then for the expression of His praise they are still sufficient. 2. It is too much for any man to take upon himself to decide how copious a system of psalmody ought to be. 3. The Book of Psalms actually contains an incomparably greater abundance and variety of matter than all the hymns which were ever composed by men.

10. 'That we have no good metrical translation of the Psalms.'
Answer.—1. Let those who think we have no good metrical translation of the psalms improve some of the versions in use, or make a better one. It is surely easier to make a good translation of God's psalms than to compose songs better than those which He has made. 2. It is better to sing, in divine worship, an imperfect translation of those songs which God has composed, than to sing the best songs which men can make. 3. *We have* a good metrical translation of the psalms. There are in the Scottish version of the psalms, it is true, some blemishes. It contains some uncouth forms of expression, and some words which are now obsolete; and its versification in many instances is far from being smooth. But, for the most part, both the phraseology and the versification are very good; and it must be allowed by those who have examined it, that its fidelity to the original Hebrew is not much, if at all, inferior to that of the prose translation of the psalms in our English Bible.

"These few observations are submitted to the judgment of the candid and intelligent reader. Though they may not be blessed as a means of reclaiming any from the practice of using human psalmody, yet if they serve to establish some in their attachment to the psalms of inspiration, the writer will not consider his labour lost. Christian worshippers will one day see eye to eye, on this, as on all other important points. In the mean time, all the fearers of God can, with confidence, commit the interests of Christ's truth, so far as they are involved in this controversy, to the management of Him who brings order out of confusion, and light out of darkness: and praying, 'Thy will be done, on earth as it is in heaven,' rest assured that very soon, in songs appointed by Jehovah's own high authority, the devout worshipper will everywhere ' give to the LORD the glory due unto His name.'

> " Praise ye the Lord ; unto him sing
>   a new song; and his praise,
> In the assembly of his saints,
>   In sweet psalms do ye raise.
>
> " Let Isr'el in his Maker joy,
>   and to him praises sing;
> Let all that Zion's children are,
>   be joyful in their KING."

PAMPHLETS ON THE PSALMODY QUESTION,

Published by JAMES JOHNSTON, Police-Place, Belfast.

THE INSPIRED PSALMS ONLY TO BE USED IN THE WORSHIP OF GOD: A Preface. By the Rev. DOCTOR MARTIN, of America. With Introduction by the Rev. THOMAS HOUSTON, D.D., Professor of Exegetical and Pastoral Theology, Belfast.

THE PSALMS AND PARAPHRASES. A SERMON by the Rev. WILLIAM JOHNSTON, of Townsend Street Church, Belfast. Price 2d.

DIVINE PSALMS AGAINST HUMAN PARAPHRASES AND HYMNS. Review of the Rev. WILLIAM JOHNSTON's Sermon on the "Psalms and Paraphrases." By the Rev. THOMAS HOUSTON, D.D.

BELFAST:—W. M'Comb, C. Aitchison, George Phillips & Sons, Alexander S. Mayne, and M. Pollock. DERRY:—R. Hamilton. DUBLIN:—D. Robertson, and Curry & Co.

www.ingramcontent.com/pod-product-compliance
Lightning Source LLC
Chambersburg PA
CBHW020249170426
43202CB00008B/292